Charleston

and the South

A Sampler of
Stories • Poetry • Recipes • Art

Compiled by
Southern Sampler Artists Colony

Southern Sampler Artists Colony Press
San Rafael • California

Copyright 2016 Southern Sampler Artists Colony. All rights reserved.

For permission to print essays, poems, art or recipes in this volume, acknowledgement is made to the holders of copyright named on pages 145-150.

Cover Art: *Mary Edna Fraser*, detail of the batik *The Ashley River*

Production and Design: *Cathleen O'Brien*

Edited by: *Nancy Alpert, Mary Brent Cantarutti, Martha Greenway, Linda Watanabe McFerrin, Catherine Pyke, Ellie Woods, Douglas Wyant*

ISBN-13: 978-1530578894
Published 2016 by Southern Sampler Artists Colony Press
San Rafael, California

Printed in the United States of America

For information about The Southern Sampler Artists Colony
visit our website: www.southernsamplerartistscolony.com

Charleston

and the South

The John Tecklenburg Trio —John Tecklenburg (keyboard),
Ann Caldwell (vocalist), George Kenny (tenor saxophone)
Photo: Bente Mirow

Charleston and the South

is dedicated to

The Heart in Art

Words . . . Images . . . Music

Inspiring ties and friendly tides of the
South Carolina Lowcountry

The Southern Sampler Artists Colony is a creative, bi-coastal community woven in belonging. Together, we discover the magic of words, colors, images, and notes set to a lazy Lowcountry beat.

Charleston and the South is our story—a story to be shared and embellished in time.

Mary Brent Cantarutti and Martha Greenway
California and South Carolina

Charleston

The South

Southern Cooking

Writers Artists Chefs

About the Contributers

Charleston is not the center of the universe, but it should be.
That is the persistent perception of many locals.

—Mark R. Jones, author of *Wicked Charleston:*
The Dark Side of the Holy City

Charleston

Photo: Bente Mirow

The Charleston Wind

Carolyn Bishop-Mcleod

April 2015

Her purpose is to break you. Her purpose is to mend you. In September her goal is quite obvious. She blatantly uses her minions, like Hugo, David, and Floyd, to push aside everything in her path. But in April, she is subtle and unpredictable. One day she shares soft breezes that lightly brush your cheek; the next day she is demanding that you find your sweater.

The Southern Sampler Artists Colony is no match for this dominatrix known as the Charleston Wind. Her sweet April pheromones perfume the air, and the Colony is held hostage with urges to experience Rhett Butler, Gullah folklore, salt marshes, Southern cooking, and Lowcountry melodies. Sometimes she snaps her whip with flashes and crashes of lightning and thunder—like the night of the greenhouse dinner at Chef David Vagasky's home—leaving the Colony breathless and tingly. Other times she gently coaxes the Colony along the salt marsh spartina, all calm and silky.

The Charleston Wind has mostly been kind to the Colony. She has not used her April breeze to force conversations about the South's original sin. But if the Colony inhales deeply enough, scents of past sins will begin to emerge. Someday her forces will push the Colony to ponder the destruction of the Civil War and to wonder about its reconstruction.

I know this because she pushed me hard in the wee hours of an April 2011 morning. She commanded me to the battery to attend the opening ceremonies of the sesquicentennial anniversary of the Civil War. At 4:30 a.m., on April 12, coinciding with the exact moment of the first shot fired in the Lowcountry, a beam of light emanating from Fort Sumter was split into two beams, signifying the division of the nation. At 6:45 a.m., while the Charleston Symphony Orchestra Brass Ensemble played "Jesus Wept", a star shell was fired over the harbor and the lights went out.

Here in this place that I love, not four miles from my childhood home, one hundred and fifty years ago, the subtle April wind helped deliver the first shot of the Civil

Charleston

War. From just off the banks of James Island, the South started a war to ensure that the enslavement of men, women, and children for economic purposes would continue. Just like Hurricane Hugo, the cruel practice of slavery left a path of destruction. But unlike Hurricane Hugo, which seemed to beg forgiveness for its outburst the very next day, the Civil War wind has been unapologetically saluted throughout the centuries. Only recently has Charleston garnered the courage to openly discuss the true reason for the Civil War—slavery. Now a mending wind has started to clear the air across the Lowcountry, sweeping away rationalizations like states' rights and Northern aggression.

The Colony will return in April. The Charleston Wind has not demanded of them a conversation about this destruction and rebirth … yet.

June 22, 2015

It is almost a week since a storm of destruction far fiercer than anyone could ever imagine hit my beloved Charleston. I did not fathom that the conversation would happen so quickly or violently. Dylann Roof killed more people than Hurricane Hugo, and his heinous actions unleashed on The Holy City a force unlike anything the world has ever seen. Yet, strangely, forgiveness is what was left in the aftermath of his actions. His path of destruction resulted in unimaginable expressions of grace, courage, and love. The families of Susie Jackson, Sharonda Coleman-Singleton, DePayne Doctor, Ethel Lance, Daniel Simmons, Rev. Clementa Pinckney, Cynthia Hurd, and Tywanza Sanders, now forever linked as the "Mother Emanuel 9", have shown us the light of the dawn after the storm. The Charleston Wind is now enveloping our nation, leading the conversation on racism with heated summer reminders and, once again, pushing aside everything in her path.

Three Haiku

Beginning light dance

Flowing channel of color

Harvests moon shadows

Sultry end of May

Morning rain mists the islands

Breath exits the womb

Ribbons of sand float

Barriers stretch and release

Adagio's breath

—*Mary Edna Fraser*

Charleston

The Scent of Tea Olive

Harlan Greene

I think many of us are heathen here in the holy city. I know I am.

With so many seductions, it's hard not to surrender to sensuality: with voluptuous visuals, the balm of breezes, and more restaurants than tastes or appetites to appease, Charleston is a city of the senses.

As for scent, many rhapsodize over the sulfurous smell of low tide. Along marshes, creeks and the battery, I have, like an asthmatic his inhaler, breathed in the deep earthy smell of pluff mud, as pungent and nose-wrinkling as wasabi. But, for my favorite, I vote for something else altogether. I'm talking about that which comes with a more gradual shift than the seas—it's the seasonal change when tides of fragrance wash down the streets. It comes after summer has burned itself out, and the palmettos rattle like dice. And it reappears when the city wakes from its winter nap in the heady resurgence of spring. From September to May, and for centuries, since Andre Michaux introduced it, tea olive has been tantalizing and delighting us. As long as I can remember, it's been intoxicating me.

If you've ever gotten a whiff of it, you understand; and if you haven't, you have my pity. If you set out to find it, however, good luck. The plant is whimsical, blooming when it will; just when you've given up or forgotten its existence, it will ambush you with the sweetest smell imaginable. Not sickly sweet, but delicate—a faintly wistful smell, ripe apricots or something as unearthly as a ghostly harpsichord or a happy memory. I can't tell you how many times I've changed my itinerary, been on the way somewhere else when waylaid by the fragrance. When it calls, I obey its summoning.

Turning corners, I'm lured on as if by a laughing lover, teasing me down tree-hung streets and shadowy allies. Here, here, it cries. Not there. Here.

When I take visitors around, they invariably stop the conversation and grab my sleeve when gales of it engulf us. "What's that?" they ask. "That ... wonderful ... smell?" They have to see what's producing it. And so the hunt is on. But finding the tea olive is not easy. You'd think the blooms would be as big and boisterous, as over-the-top as a magnolia. Like that of an overly perfumed woman, those May and June blooms are the languorous smell of summer setting in, delicious yes, but debilitating. Tea olive, on the other hand, is demure and dainty, as shy as a single house turned to one side, ladylike and discreet. The tiny white blooms, smaller than BBs, cluster together as if hiding under holly-like green leaves.

And what makes it harder to spot is that it's only once you've passed down-wind that you notice it, prompting that sudden lurch to a stop and backtracking as if you've heard your name called, discovered the square root of wonderful, or remembered something perplexing. And when the tiny unassuming blossoms are found and pointed out, my friends express their disbelief. How can it be? It's the mathematician's and theologian's riddle. The whole is so much vaster than the sum of its parts. How can something that small cast such a huge spell?

I cannot answer. I'm no botanist. Just a bystander groping for analogies. I know if it were music, it would be that of the pied piper, something to make me follow it almost unwillingly. Sometimes I wonder if it might serve as a symbol of the city itself. Charleston is such a tiny corner of the universe, but the power it can exert on the unsuspecting is as tremendous and oversized as is scent to the tea olive. We who wander into the city's spell are often taken unawares, seduced and beguiled and pressed, drugged, into its orbit.

After seasons of obeisance to the tea olive, I understand the sermon it preaches on the street. The gift—or blessing—of its scent comes unbidden; we do not deserve it, nor can we cause it. It comes when it will, and like the rest of life's sudden and unearned joys, it's best not to question; just breathe deep and give in till it vanishes, haunting us with its sweetness and evanescence.

To this heathen, it is Heaven scent.

Charleston

Breaking Day

The sun slips into the Lowcountry sky—

a pancake stirred in earth's kitchen,

served up in orange flames,

a divine concoction offered to day.

Which way to turn?

West, I decide.

My shadow, a wispy being set free in the angled light,

stretches tall and flat, pressed into life.

Heel toe, heel toe: I step with purpose.

Promise slithers up my spine,

life's frame spreads out in waves.

What flows will be.

I pick up a reed.

Drawing in the sand, a heart shape emerges

one stroke at a time.

I draw a line through the center,

one side for light,

one side for dark,

pray for balance in all.

Breathe, the ocean whispers,

breathe.

— *Mary Brent Cantarutti*

*Compost in my Shoe—Dirt Works Incubator Farm,
John's Island, South Carolina*   Photo: Toni Carreiro

Charleston

High Notes in the Lowcountry:
The Charleston Jazz Initiative

Catherine Pyke

Jazz at high noon! It's The Mezz, located above Sermet's Downtown, King Street, in the heart of historical Charleston. I share a table with other San Francisco Bay Area writers attending the annual Southern Sampler Artists Colony workshop. Along with local patrons, we have gathered to celebrate and support the Charleston Jazz Initiative. I look around the room with its exposed brick walls, heart pine floors, and small tables covered with crisp white cloths—a bud vase containing a single red rose in the center of each. It's easy to imagine that I have found myself in a well-appointed living room, now filled with chatting folk eagerly anticipating the arrival of the Quentin Baxter Quintet, who typically work into the wee hours and rise late in the day. I sip my sweet tea—a concession to Southern taste—and wait, my curiosity piqued. A devotee of jazz, I know little about its origins in the Lowcountry. In my mind, jazz belongs to New Orleans.

An undercurrent of excitement sweeps the room when Quentin, a native Charlestonian, drummer, and founder of the quintet, steps on stage and introduces his fellow musicians. A slight man with dreadlocks and an engaging smile, Quentin acknowledges that this is indeed an unusual performance time, but from the first notes, it seems that the musicians have been playing as one, night or day, for years.

The riff begins . . . notes gently offered and received . . . circling back whole. Charlton Singleton, the trumpeter-composer, explains that his song "Delicate" came to him while untangling his three-year-old daughter's hair. "Now she's twenty and won't let me anywhere near her hair. Time passes too quickly," he says.

Mesmerized by the music and stories, I vow to research the Lowcountry jazz legacy, but never would have guessed that some of its development traces back to a Charleston orphanage.

Later I learn that the Jenkins Orphanage bands began with the Reverend Daniel

Joseph Jenkins, a Baptist minister. In December 1891, while loading timber for his wood business, Jenkins stumbled across four homeless boys who were warming themselves by a fire. Taking pity on the boys, he took them home with him and appealed to his Baptist congregation to establish a charitable association to assist these and other orphaned children. The resulting organization—established as the Orphan Aid Society and later known as the Jenkins Orphanage—became one of the oldest private, black orphanages in the nation.

From 1894 on, Jenkins' instructors used music as a learning tool, focusing on wind instruments to develop young boys' lung capacity. Soon they became well known for the high trumpet playing style. Indeed, many Charleston musicians learned their craft through the Jenkins Orphanage bands' technique, attracting the attention of Duke Ellington, Count Basie, Cab Holloway, and Lionel Hampton, who recruited them for their bands and ensembles in the Golden Age of Swing. Side men, the Jenkins players could always be relied upon to read music and exhibit a fine sense of style. As one alumnus put it, "During the day, we played the music as it was written. But at night, we had jam sessions like you wouldn't believe."

That day at the Mezz the music was fresh and alive, just like one of those jam sessions.

Charleston

My Partner in Time, My Little Joy

To the Quentin Baxter Quintet

4/17/13

My *drumming* pulse

    thumps rhythmic warmth

while deep in my *base*

    my heartstrings strum.

My body sings in counterpoint

    the *key* to love's sweet melody.

Anoint the *horn* of happiness

    and blast the news aloud

My life is blessed with *sacks* of joy

    since you were borne of play's caress.

                  — *Nancy Alpert*

Southern Girls

Anne Sigmon

Some people go to priests, others to poetry, I to my friends.
—Virginia Woolf, *The Waves*

The toes of my sandals caught on the tumble-down sidewalk as I hurried along Calhoun Street, dodging cracks and tree roots, toward the Francis Marion Hotel. This get-together with Barbara had been my idea; I didn't want to be late.

I took a deep breath. Old Charleston smelled of sea salt, river marsh, and antique brick. The azaleas stole the show, strutting their crimson blooms here and all over the South every April. But it was the sticky sweet fragrance of gardenias and the musky scent of boxwood hedges that carried me back to my youth—to three sultry Carolina coming-of-age years when Barbara was my first best friend.

Not long after those years of our acquaintance, I'd left the South and carved a blue-state life firmly rooted on the west coast. Now my family—who'd all held firm to southern soil—was shrinking fast. My mother's memory, attacked by Alzheimer's, was shredding like some old kitchen curtain hung too long in the sun. She was the last of her generation, my only link to what came before.

Maybe it had been some nameless longing for southern connections that led me to accept an invitation to spend a week in Charleston at the Southern Sampler Artists Colony. I'd intended only to mingle with the colony's artists, sip sweet tea, listen to the cicadas in the dew of an evening, and hope for lightning bugs and far thunder. Maybe I'd also sneak in a Dairy Queen cone. But the day after I signed up for the trip, as I sat at my desk mulling over possible flights, it came to me, not so much a thought as an unequivocal, almost audible, imperative: Go early, see Barbara.

This sudden longing to reconnect with my junior high school best friend thrummed with a nervous urgency that belied the facts. Though we'd stayed in touch over the years via occasional letters (hers; she wasn't partial to email), once-in-a-blue-moon phone calls (mine), and Christmas cards bursting with news and kid pictures, I hadn't laid eyes on her actual person in almost forty years.

Charleston

In the late sixties, ours had been an intense bonding full of early-teen angst about everything from our mouse brown-hair (hers too curly, mine too straight) to parents (my impatient mom, her strict dad), music (she was talented like my mother, I aspired), and, most of all, boys.

We'd met at the school bus stop on the first day of school a month after my family moved to Greensboro, North Carolina—our new split-level a few blocks from her family's rambling ranch.

On steamy summer afternoons we'd retreat to the cool downstairs of one house or the other and swoon to teen-longing love songs like "Unchained Melody" or the Beach Boys' "Warmth of the Sun," and weigh the relative dreaminess quotients of John, Paul, or George. Ringo was nobody's idea of a heartthrob. When we were sure no one else was home, we'd drop the needle over and over again, trying to suss out the words to "House of the Rising Sun."

On some summer afternoons, Barbara's mom drove us to Beach Blanket movies in her baby-blue Mustang. On the way home we often stopped at Fordham's Drug Store. Sitting on green vinyl stools, Barbara and I slurped coffee ice cream sodas and played at sophistication. Then we'd walk four blocks to shop for brush rollers and bobby pins at Woolworth's where, just six years earlier, local college students had staged a peaceable lunch-counter sit-in that marked one of the first salvos of the American civil-rights movement.

The next year Barbara met Billy and fell hard, and permanently, in love. A wiry carrot top with braces, Billy had a waggish sense of humor and a penchant for mischievous fun. He also rode a motorcycle—the perfect profile to drive Barbara's father mad. So Billy courted Barbara at my house under the more tolerant, but still watchful eye of my dad.

Now, against all odds, Barbara and Billy were still together. After a bustle of emails and a few euphoric phone calls, we'd agreed to meet for an afternoon while I was in Charleston.

But once I'd made the arrangements, a sliver of doubt gnawed at the edge of my excitement. What did I expect? We were so different now. Barbara and Billy had moved to a small town and raised two daughters who, as teenagers, loved cheerleading and Disneyland. In all the photos of their growing up years, they remained the spitting image of Barbara—the ringleted hair, the sweeping smile upturned at the corners. Their family's travels were strictly on four wheels as Barbara did not like to fly. In contrast, I'd taken my rollercoaster love life west where, failing to have children, I threw my energies into career and travel to wild and dangerous places. I fretted. What would we have to talk about?

A black-suited bellman held the door as I dashed into the Francis Marion Hotel, a still-graceful relic of jazz-age Charleston. I slowed my pace as I walked up the stairs into the sweeping lobby, patting my hair and adjusting my long batik duster that tended to go cattywampus when I hurried. I scanned the room, past the worn Persian-style carpet, the grand piano, and coffee-colored damask sofas, until I saw Barbara perched like a debutante on the edge of a Federal walnut settee. Her hair was a glorious silver boy-cut. She wore a chic black and white tunic, leggings, and tiny patent-leather ballet flats trimmed in the same red as her lipstick. Billy sat in an overstuffed chair, wearing jeans and wrap-around sunglasses that hung casually around his neck. His once flame-red mop-top was now a distinguished gray.

They jumped up when they saw me and I swooped in for a group hug. Forty years fell away in that moment of shared embrace. I sat down next to Barbara and we all began talking at once. We laughed about the old days, the time my father caught us smoking at the deli, what happened to this friend or that. We talked about kids, grandkids, jobs, retirement. Billy's never-quelled loved of fast cars. Barbara's foray into local theater. We traversed the years in photo books Barbara pulled from a tote bag— birthday parties, graduations, christening of grandkids, then digital pictures from my iPad—trekking through jungles, riding camels across the desert mountains, Christmas with Jack's daughters and our grandkids.

"I never got to be a mom, but when Jack's girls started having children, I finally got to be a grandma," I said.

"You surely did." The velvety southern lilt of Barbara's voice reminded me so much of my father.

That's the only time the talk turned solemn, when we remembered our parents,

Charleston

all gone now except my mother, who was fast on her way. Barb's father, a former football player, had faced the long, slow death of Alzheimer's. She shared some tips with me about what I might face with my mom along this sad road.

Seeking to lighten the mood and stave off hunger, we moved to the hotel's restaurant, where we devoured Lowcountry favorites: fried green tomatoes, shrimp and grits, crab cakes, and pimento cheese. With iced tea, of course.

After lunch we walked around the neighborhood, past the gothic revival sanctuary of St. Matthews Church; past historic pink stucco buildings with green shutters and white plantation blinds; down Vanderhorst, an old residential block of Charleston "single houses," homes with Doric columns and wide porches or "piazzas" to catch the breeze. As we circled the block back to Marion Park and the hotel, we all knew it was time for them to go. We stopped for a series of photos under a magnolia tree and said reluctant goodbyes.

I hadn't had enough. As I watched Barbara and Billy head off to their car, I was sad that our visit was over. I wanted to rest a while longer in the comfort of a sheltered past with old friends. I had other friends now, good ones. But Barbara and Billy were my first best friends, who'd shared the crucible of young adolescence—who'd known my parents when they were young with so much life left to live. I didn't want to let that go.

Ole Power, the Buzzard, the Possum, the Boar, the Rooster, the Catfish and the Ant

Sharon Cooper-Murray

One day as Ole Power sat in his old chair he heard a loud argument between the Buzzard, Possum, Boar, Rooster and Catfish. They were arguing over food. You see, all of them arrived at the river at the same time and each of them saw a piece of meat lying on the edge of the water. The meat looked delicious because they were all very hungry.

The Buzzard said, "Y'all know I saw that piece of meat first from way up in the sky so it's my meat."

The Possum said, "No, I saw it first. I saw the Leopard when he dragged it to the edge of the river last night so I actually saw it first, and it's mine."

The Boar said, "I saw it first. I was there when the Leopard first got the meat because it was a much bigger piece than what we see right now. So I saw it first; it's MINE."

The Catfish said, "When the Leopard dragged it in the water and starting eating, I grabbed a piece and swam away. So it is mine. I already ate a piece."

The Rooster said, "No it's mine. I walked up while Leopard was eating the meat and ate some with him, and when he was finished, I asked him if could I have the rest of the meat and he said 'yes'. So it's mine."

All of them said they had a right to the meat. Buzzard squawked, Possum scratched his head, Boar grunted, Rooster clucked and Catfish splashed around in the water trying to figure out what to do to solve their problem.

While they were thinking about what to do, the Ant walked up and in a sharp high-pitched voice said, "It's mine, and I will beat the first one of you that tries to get a piece."

The Buzzard, the Possum, the Boar, the Rooster and the Catfish laughed and laughed until their stomachs began to hurt. Finally the Boar grunted and said, "You are the smallest among us and you want to fight one of us? I could step on you and squash you."

Buzzard said, "I could pick you up in my mouth and fly high in the sky and drop you, and when you hit the ground you would splatter."

Possum said, "I could lie down on you and squeeze you and that would be the end of you."

Rooster said, "I could pick you up with my beak and snap you into pieces."

Catfish said, "I could splash water on you and drown you."

The Ant stood up on his hind legs and poked his chest out and said, "I challenge all of you and I know I can win so DON'T TOUCH MY MEAT."

Once again they all started to argue over the meat lying on the edge of the water. They argued the rest of the day and all through the night. The following morning they were still arguing until the Ant stood up and said, "Even though the meat is mine, I'll let you all have the rest of it," and Ant walked away.

The Buzzard, the Possum, the Boar, the Rooster and the Catfish rushed toward the meat and when they got to it there was nothing but bones. Buzzard, Possum, Boar, Rooster and the Catfish were very confused and wondered what could have happened to the meat. They were there, by or in the river, the whole time and didn't see any other animals that could have eaten the meat. What could have happened to the meat?

Then suddenly in the far distance they all heard a tiny sharp, high-pitched loud voice. It was Ant and he said, "Hey, Mr. Buzzard, Mr. Possum, Mr. Boar, Mr. Rooster and Mr. Catfish, I guess by now you see all the meat is gone, ha-ha-ha. You see, while all of you were arguing, all 10,000 of my brothers came and removed every single piece of meat from the edge of the river. So the next time somebody my size walks up to you and tells you if you try to take their stuff they will beat you, you will remember this day 'cause size don't mean nothing if you learn how to use you head."

Buzzard, Possum, Boar, Rooster and Catfish looked at each other then Boar angrily said, "WE SHOULD GO AFTER THEM AND TAKE THE MEAT BACK!"

Rooster slowly said, "I know we are bigger and stronger than the Ant, but he did say he called 10,000 of them. I think we should just let them have the meat.

One by one they all said, "Rooster, I think you are right; we should let them keep the meat."

Ole Power considered the lesson the animals learned from the dispute over the meat, and it brought a big smile to his face as he slowly leaned back to rest in his big chair.

The Gullah Lady   Photo: Bente Mirow

Charleston

The Gullah Lady Reveals Herself

Maureen Dixon

"Da dey honner jine en wid dem dat gut a good haat, dats da day honner meet a friend."

"The day you meet someone with a good heart is the day you meet a friend."

Sharon Cooper-Murray is widely known in the greater Charleston, South Carolina area as the Gullah Lady. That's how I came to know her. Dressed in an ankle-length, blue, two-piece cotton dress and a head wrap, she reminds many Southerners of the women who cared for them or their parents when they were young—a wise and beloved cook, housekeeper or nanny. As the Gullah Lady, Sharon performs for groups large and small, sharing the stories, art, wisdom and language of this little known cultural group. The Gullah people, enslaved West Africans, brought their skills in growing rice by using the tides to the plantations in the South Carolina Lowcountry.

The Gullah Lady is entertaining, engaging, and interactive with her audiences and lots of fun. She is larger than life. I'm not from the South and, as the eldest child of seven in a third-generation California family, I've never had a nanny, but through Sharon I learned a lot about an unfamiliar culture and one that fascinated me. What was Sharon's purpose in bringing this character to life? What was she trying to teach us?

I met with her one afternoon on Sullivan's Island. Sharon was not in costume. A striking woman, full of laughter and surprise even when not on stage, Sharon wore a simple turquoise shift and a long scarf with a turquoise and lavender print. Her hair was yellow-blond and cut short to frame her oval face. Her enunciation was impeccable and easy to understand, very different from her persona's Gullah patois.

Having grown up in the suburbs outside of Los Angeles, I was captivated to learn that Sharon was raised in a small town in Florence County called Lake City—in a house that had been abandoned. Some believe a ghost had cleared out the residents. Before the supposed ghost came, the people farmed tobacco and cotton as well as some soybeans and corn. Sharon's family had lots of animals—mules, cows, pigs and dogs.

She loved those dogs, and as an only child spent many happy hours playing with them. Her parents sharecropped the farm, as did many of their neighbors. Her daddy and his brother also owned a barbershop in town. "I grew up around the farm and in and out of that barbershop," Sharon said with mischief in her eyes, "and I can tell you that men gossip as much as women, no matter what they say."

Her mother was a seamstress who made church dresses for Sharon and clothes for herself and other people. Sharon looked forward to harvest season, when her cousins would come live with them. When she was small, she and her little cousin would pick up the tobacco leaves that fell onto the floor of the barn and bring them back to the men who were tying the leaves into big bundles.

"My mother was the most important influence in my life," Sharon continued. "She was always asking me, 'What college are you going to?' I'd answer a different school each time, but that question put it into my head that I was going to college." Sharon's mother became very ill the last year Sharon was in high school. When the doctor gave her an appointment six months out instead of just a few weeks, everyone in the family knew that meant she had less than six months to live.

"Mommy would call me into her room and say, 'When I die,' and then she'd tell me something important. Once she told me about how to understand when people are 'coming at you good and when they aren't.' Another time she said, 'No one can stop you from having what you want in life. They can make it very difficult for you, but they can't stop you.' She was fabulous. She knew I might not understand what she was saying then, but as I grew older and experienced more of life, I would, and she was right."

"My grandmother was wise like that, too. She'd tell us, 'If you ever get in trouble, before you call anyone in the family you'd better have done every possible thing you can think of to get yourself out of that trouble, because when you were having fun and got yourself into that situation you didn't invite us then.'"

I had recognized that same strength and no-nonsense attitude in Sharon; they were some of the qualities I enjoyed about her. She and I just seemed to hit it off, even though our beginnings were so different. "I think our spirits are the same," Sharon said when I asked why she thought we got along so well.

Sharon did fulfill her mother's dream. She studied English, speech and drama at Knoxville College for two years and at the University of Tennessee at Knoxville for the last two. When she graduated, she began teaching school, but found she didn't enjoy it. After stints as a recruiter with the Department of Labor, which she did enjoy, and the Department of Commerce where she supervised staff for eleven counties, and a brief respite as a stay-at-home mom with her three children—"I got tired of baby-talk"—Sharon wanted something different.

"I conducted an oral history project on John's Island and Wadmalaw Island. It took a year and a half. The elders loved to tell stories about their parents and grand-parents. They'd share their memories, crafts, and food customs, all in a rich language filled with African and Creole rhythms. I'd share their stories with my friends. One day a friend talked me into telling my stories at a festival in front of an audience. A tall man with light brown hair came up to me afterwards and told me I was a natural born storyteller. He started talking about the industry of storytelling. I interrupted him, 'You mean people will pay me for telling stories?' That was the epiphany I had that eventually led to the Gullah Lady."

Sharon started telling more stories on stage, and the audiences loved her. She always dressed in a full antebellum costume of a skilled craftswoman to differentiate herself and help create an atmosphere for her tales. She also spent a year working as the black history coordinator at Middleton Place to learn the history of the plantations as well as how to weave and spin and other artisan skills. She now incorporates these skills into her performance art and storytelling.

Along the way Sharon took up textile art based on the rag quilting techniques that she learned from the elder women. "The art form was dying out, and I wanted to carry on the tradition." But as it took nine women three months to make a quilt, Sharon adapted the techniques to modernize the uses of the art form and make it uniquely her own. She now makes wall-hangings, table runners, purses and clothing using rag quilt-ing methods. In 2001 she formed the Community Rag Quilting Preservation Initiative (CRQPI), now a non-profit project of the Palmetto Project, to preserve the indigenous textile traditions of the rice plantation culture of South Carolina.

As I listened, I felt Sharon was teaching a lot more than crafts and history. She was a bridge builder among people of different cultures. Sharon confirmed my theory. "I hammer on the importance of learning about the culture of a group you're going to be in all the time. You find out that we are all doing the same things, even if we do them differently. I'll give you an example. A friend of mine had only performed for black audiences, so she didn't know what to expect when she was asked to perform for her first white audience. The history of black social gatherings is call and response. In a black church, the congregation calls back to the preacher, 'Yes, Reverend. Go ahead, preacher,' like that. So my friend starts performing and on her break says to me, 'They hate me. You could hear a pin drop in there.' I did a devilish thing and just let her stew on it. When she finished her performance the audience stood up and clapped like crazy. That's how she learned.

"When you understand the culture you are going into you don't get offended by others, and you don't offend them either. As a performer you have to show a good example of how to interact. If someone offends me, I tell them a story that is the flip side. If people like your story, they will listen and eventually see the wisdom that is behind it. I've connected with people when I didn't even understand a word they were saying. But everyone, no matter what language they speak or where they are from, understands a smile."

As we concluded our interview, I was smiling as broadly as Sharon and knew I had made a new friend. We understood each other just fine.

The Gullah Lady   Photo: Bente Mirow

Twist Dolls

For Sharon Cooper-Murray

Indigo, indigo

boo-hag blue,

I'm gonna put

a spell on you.

Make a yarn doll

and tie with a twist

all of the things

you've feared

and wished.

Closer and closer

and closer they come:

evil and good …

now, you choose one.

—*Linda Watanabe McFerrin*

The Gullah Lady   Photo: Marueen Dixon

Yah Fut Tah Crooked

Sharon Cooper-Murray   a.k.a. The Gullah Lady

See dis yah time long time back yonda de roosta ain been de fuss thing fah git up en de mornin e bun dah hen. En dah ting beena git up en da fuss ting he da do, dah ting benna staat fah dig en de dut en say shaaz, dig some roung en say shaaz. Den dah ting beena look roung e see de hoss had shaaz, da ting beena look en see de cow add e shaaz dah ting beena see de durty down pig add e shaaz. I want fah know why me ain dah gut no shaaz.

So ting beena jump up en down, en jump up en down en say shaaz, fah dig en de dut en say shaaz. But see dah roosta been mad, den fo day break clean dah roosta beena git up fuss, dah ting beena fly pond top de highest post, an when he git up dey, soon as dah hen fah step out e doe Dah roosta beena say if honna want fah no why honna ain gut shaaz, I'll tell yah why honna ain da gut no shoes cause yah fut tah **crooked**.

Sound of the Rooster

In other words—the story's called Your Foot Too Crooked.

You see one time the hen was the first to get up in the morning, not the rooster. The hen would get up, and as soon as she got up, the first thing she'd start saying was "shoes" and dig in the dirt and say "shoes". Cause, you see, when she looked around the horse had shoes, the cow had shoes, even the dirty down pig had shoes.

So ee wanted to know why me ain't got no shoes. So she'd dig in the dirt and say "shoes, shoes." Well, the rooster would get angry, so one morning the rooster got up first and flew to the highest post and soon as the hens step out of their house, the rooster turned and said, "Old hens, if you want to know why you have no shoes, well, I'll tell why you have no shoes, cause YOUR FOOT TOO CROOKED."

Meditations on a Baby Blanket

Mary Jean (MJ) Pramik

Henry Oliver Ng is now four years old. His "baby blanket," meant to welcome and greet his entry onto this planet, finally lies across his toddler bed, complete, beautiful but about two and a half years late. Here's why.

Henry's "covers"—as he calls his blanket—is a multi-thread, cool-green cotton yarn. It endured an evolutionary process over the past three years. For what seemed like three centuries, I crocheted and crocheted right to left, then left to right—same single stitch broken with a surprise double stitch every ten rows or so—repeating the wrist motion, in-out-loop-pull through…next the turn of the copper hook, the tight loop and final gentle through motion.

After months of what felt like slogging through Jell-O, I considered hiring a surrogate "Grammy" to finish the project. I'm usually "on the run," so sitting still and inventing the "pattern" (very funny that word) as I went along, really was a stressor. Instead of the project providing relaxation, my body tensed as I picked up the half completed love blanket. If I could have sat in front of the television and *zened* into crocheting, it might have been completed earlier. I scrambled to write the "American Novel" (I dropped "Great" the first five years into the project), so Henry's warm cuddly gift from his grandmother had to wait. Luckily he lives in San Diego, California, where it's warm.

Last April, however, I met inspiration, a pulling sensation that demanded that I finish what I started. At the Southern Sampler Artists Colony, I met the Gullah Lady Sharon (thank you!), who showed up with her rag quilt. I fingered the strips of cloth she spread all over the table. Sharon's instructions on how to weave these random bits of fabric that were *us* into this rag quilt awoke an energy in me, a drive to get it done. I now understood creative space, an opening up of a place inside that stopped the *musts* of this world and allowed what should become. Eureka! I knew how to finish off the edges to "hide" the "errors" in the blanket. Henry would love it: solid green variegated tight-blend yarn edged in a multifarious soft alpaca for fringe.

During each crochet movement, I thought of Henry. He grew from a staring new-born to a crawler then a dancer, and now a talker, as I sat under the growing blanket. Just over a year ago he became a big brother to little sis Charlotte Iris.

Walking into the sunrise on those Sullivan's Island mornings at the Southern Sampler Artists Colony (SSAC) opened my heart to the "finishing" task of the creative process. Being a part of this artists' group, the crazy-hearted jumble of southern comfort and acceptance that explodes on the Island each April, gently nudged me to complete my labor of love in our tizzy-paced world. I look forward to next year's SSAC to prod me to wrap up Charlotte's quilt (Hawaiian green-leafed backing with multifarious colored squares of cloth collected over two decades on the Pacific Islands) ahead of her second birthday.

Photo: Mary Jean (MJ) Pramik

Looking for the Dead

Linda Watanabe McFerrin

The air is thick with water, with our collective sweat—enough to rewind hair into corkscrews, soak it flat against damp foreheads, slick thick necks with perspiration—enough to drown you. The bugs know this and they drone on and on about it, like tiny lawnmowers cutting through the music of our talk. They are mad with desire. They circulate about our heads like thorny crowns, kiss our foreheads and our faces, leave welts. There is salt in the nearby sea, salt in the air in this coastal town, and I taste sweat when I raise my hand to my lips.

Around us the ground of Magnolia Cemetery seems to swell in the heat. I've lost the others. They have drifted off among the headstones … and lovely headstones they are. The dead get such a celebration here in the South. They get respect, trumpets and drums; sometimes they get a parade. So why don't they just stay dead?

Lately, I've been reading a lot about the dead. It's an obsession, actually. I've had quite a lot of intercourse with spirits. I don't mean sexually—incubi and succubi are not my thing—I mean I've had no small amount of interaction, visitation, and myste-rious communication with the departed, what with so many of my loved ones (infant daughter, thirteen-year-old brother, younger sister, youthful friends, and all my fam-ily elders) on the other side. Let's just say the wall between me and those who have passed is more like a curtain, and a flimsy one at that.

Apparently here in the South Carolina Lowcountry, this is not unusual. This is, after all, Poe country, and I am a dyed-in-the-wool Edgar Allan Poe fan. I've also written a novel about zombies, which entailed quite a bit of research into African theological systems and their influences in the New World. In her book, *Talking to the Dead: Religion, Music, and Lived Memory Among Gullah/Geechee Women*, notable scholar and ethnographer LeRhonda S. Manigault-Bryant investigates the manner in which Gullah/Geechee women integrate the dead into their lives, combining Christian and folk tradition in ways that create a rich and textured blend of pragmatism and belief that ties spirit and the community of the dead to the day-to-day needs of the living. Through her conversations with seven women, she explores the more fluid perception of time, space, and being that is unique to the blended origins and backgrounds of their communities, and she explains how this perception enhances lives and provides support to a population that has suffered and endured much. Manigault-Bryant sheds light on how the dead are conjured and consulted, provoked and praised and how they are always present: teaching, warning, punishing and forgiving.

Oddly, this is one of the things I love most about the South as I am coming to discover it. I love a place where ceilings are painted blue to let the haints know where they are not welcome. I love a place where ancestors and other deceased loved ones are not only revered but also asked to weigh in on significant matters—a world where they actually answer. And I love a place where interaction with the dead is not always a dark one, although I do believe a boo hag took a little ride on my chest one hot South Carolina night. My roommate, who interfered and subsequently ended up in the emergency room of a local hospital, will testify to some very strange goings on! And I did discover that a blue sombrero (the only blue thing handy) placed at the crack beneath a door can have a prophylactic effect when it comes to unwanted nightly visitors of the ghostly variety.

Mostly I love a place where the membranes are permeable; where the balance that keeps us seemingly safe and secure and that simultaneously limits our perceptions, is consistently threatened; where I can so easily give myself up to the heat and the headstones and the insect coloratura and take a stroll with the dead, while the living amble off amid other landscapes and slip through other doors.

Charleston

Seeking: Southern Gentleman

Nancy Alpert

I spotted the young hunk leaning against the bar at The Gritz, a popular hang-out in downtown Charleston. Tall, muscular, dark-haired. All I desired was for him to drawl all over me. I sauntered over and cooed, "Hiya, handsome."

At least, so went my fantasy.

In reality, my peri-menopausal hormones had done the speaking that April morning during my yoga class. They salaciously demanded an "opened leg" pose instead of the "crossed knee as if at a bar" pose our teacher had suggested.

Clearly, I had some learnin' to do about Southern manners.

That same morning all signs had pointed to a saucy adventure in Charleston. I'd been intimately caressed in my dreams and had awakened to an email from a guy named *Hittero4* from the online dating site, OKCupid.

"I was caught by your page and could bear (sic) the beauty you wore and the lovely smile on your face so I had to kindly write," he wrote. His non-command of English skills unsettled me. His unfortunate choice of photos displayed a menacing, large and unfriendly face. Our match rate was a lowly ten percent. I passed.

I was due for romance. A writing conference in San Miguel de Allende two months prior had rekindled the dormant flame of a libido stamped out by my controlling ex-husband. I'd hinted at my dalliance to Linda, our writing coach.

"Did you have an assignation in Mexico?" she asked. I figured she meant a paid writing assignment, since she snagged a lot of those.

"No," I answered, then paused and asked for the definition.

"My dear, it's a more cultured way to say a 'fling'," she replied.

Clearly, I had some learnin' to do in English as well as about manners.

I decided that my Charleston assignation, should I choose to accept it, would have to involve a Southern Gentleman. I'd had enough of guys from the West Coast and Northeast. To date, my primary boyfriends had either been unemployed and under-mature, lawyers or should-a-been lawyers. All weighed a bit heavy on the narcissistic scale. And my ex? Well, let's just say there's truth to the joke, "Why is divorce expensive?" (pause) "Because it's worth it!" (applause).

In search of my Southern sample, I changed my OKCupid location to Sullivan's Island and set the match parameters to Jewish men between fifty and fifty-nine. OK Cupid replied, "This is embarrassing, we didn't find anyone."

I mused about the emotional capabilities of a search engine, then let it off the hook and took Jewish out of my requirements. I kept my height requirements (5'9"- 6'3") and awaited the responses. I didn't have to wait long. First came *Lowcountryman#1's* profile, which bragged about his tongue's talent in performing something "unmentionable." I renamed him *#Lowlifeman* and passed. *Zingman2* posed by his shiny motorcycle in one photo and proudly dangled two sizable fish in another. I questioned our compatibility. When *Undercover4me* popped up in all his bare-chested glory on my new high definition iPhone 6 screen, I aborted my online search.

I retreated to fantasy once again.

My Southern Gentleman will be Pierce Brosnan-handsome, and his perfect tongue will be used to twill his Southern brogue.

"Darlin', you look lovely," he'll murmur when he comes to call.

My face will glow in the light of the downtown street lamps, my peach chiffon gown flowing in the spring breeze.

We'll dine at a fine four-star establishment, drinking one another in. He'll comment on my eyes and my dark lashes. After sipping a mint julep or two, we will stroll, arm in arm, through George Washington Square behind City Hall. My gent, of course, will make no reference to the statue of George, with its hint of an erection hiding in the folds of his bronze trousers. I, of course, will make no mention of its minute-man size. Naturally, I'll be wearing my new "foundation" garment, a brassiere I'd purchased from a shop near Charleston Place on the advice of a beautifully-endowed South Carolina native.

Charleston

Some time later—hours or maybe moments—the sight of my ample and unfettered bosom will inspire him to whisper into the nape of my neck, "I find something about you in every moment that entices me." Then, of course, he'll drawl all over me.

Unfortunately, all week my Southern Gentleman eluded me, though I did my best siren call. One night, my group of women friends tried out a new 'in' place outside of downtown, named Edmund Oast. I sauntered up and down the length of the crowded bar, my new "foundation" garment proudly supporting my efforts. It almost made my teal cotton yoga shirt look like it was from Victoria Secret instead of from Costco. But alas, no tall, muscular, dark-haired Pierce look-a-like looked back at me. Instead, I sat down at my table of full of supportive women and satisfied myself by chatting up Jason, our eager, goateed waiter sporting a red gingham, button-down shirt.

We conversed between courses that included Brussels sprouts, pickled shrimp and peanut butter beer. I suspected Jason was a gent because he offered to drive us home if we ordered too much alcohol.

I asked Jason point-blank if he was a Southern Gentleman.

He answered, "Yes, Ma'am." I knew I was on the right track.

"What makes you a Southern Gentleman?" I questioned.

"My mama," he said, proudly, and with no hesitation.

Each of my boyfriends definitely had "issues" with their mothers, often "loving them, but not "liking" them. I mentally put "mother love" back on my list of dating musts.

"But how would you define a Southern Gentleman?" I persisted.

Jason thought a quick minute, then answered, "He is someone who puts others first and treats everyone well, *especially* women."

I thanked him and noted (regrettably) a dearth of men who fit that definition in my dating history.

Clearly, I had some learnin' to do about Southern Belles.

Photo: Toni Carreiro

Come forth into the light of things,

let nature be your teacher.

—William Wordsworth

Pen & Ink Drawing from Magnolia Plantation

Ancient Camellias (pre-1900) are a specialty at the Magnolia Plantation. Not only did it introduce over 150 cultivars of Japonica to America from the 1840's to 1940's, it has organized and implemented a world-wide search for Ancient Camellias which are in threat of extinction.

—Cathleen O'Brien

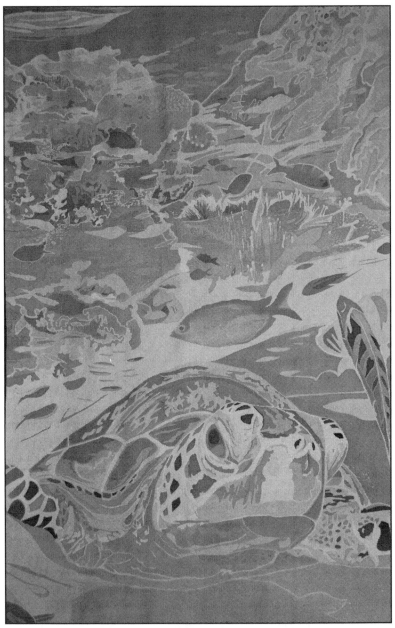

Mary Edna Fraser, detail from batik "Great Barrier Reef"   Photo: Cheryl Armstrong

Soaring with Mary Edna

Unity Barry

I look upward to see silk banners flying high overhead in vibrant splendor. Master batik artist Mary Edna Fraser has created visual odes to the earth, the oceans and the heavens using silk, wax and fabric dye. It's fitting to gaze upward to view her work because much of it was inspired when she looked down while flying in an open cockpit airplane piloted by her brother. I'm standing in Charleston's City Gallery at Waterfront Park, where the entire space is devoted to a celebration of her art. The exhibit is aptly titled *Above Between Below*. Her geographically-oceanographically- and astrophysically-inspired works have hung and been draped from the ceilings and walls of museums around the country, including the Smithsonian. She employs her unique manipulation of ancient techniques and modern technology to take viewers on magical journeys. Her banners transport us to worlds few of us get to visit. Sometimes she takes us above the stratosphere to perceive the universe through the Hubble telescope. Sometimes she takes us into deep and mysterious ocean floors never plumbed before by an artist, male or female. Sometimes she directs our gaze to the wondrous maze of waterways and barrier islands of South Carolina and beyond.

Her smile infectious, her gray-blue eyes twinkling with enthusiasm, Mary Edna Fraser's passion for truth and beauty pervades every piece she creates. She blends a prodigious scientific knowledge with gifted creativity to confront us with the beauty of our world. And to confront us with what we are close to losing.

As a graduate of the San Francisco Art Institute and an historical novelist whose writings focus on women artists, I am entralled by Mary Edna Fraser's batiks. I can't help thinking that to a new and uninformed viewer wandering into her show, her work might seem abstract. The sinuous forms of meandering rivers and erratic coastlines, of stars and heavenly bodies, and the seemingly alien life inhabiting the depths of our seas are rendered in vibrant colors. In this day of satellite images of earth, aerial photographs of our "big blue marble" seem almost familiar. It's Mary Edna's creative vision, however, that translates those photographs into an almost mystical beauty.

In the preface to *A Celebration of the World's Barrier Islands* by Orrin Pilkey and illustrated with her batiks she states, "It is difficult to capture what I feel when I'm flying over shifting islands, gaining altitude, descending to photograph a moment of visual poetry. The snaking of tidal creeks, the straight line of the Intracoastal Waterway, the abstract quality of our planet as seen from the air is intriguing. The scientific and visual variety of the Earth's barrier islands has proved to be astounding."

Sitting with Mary Edna in a Charleston Restaurant, I ask her what her influences were, especially since her work is unlike any other I've seen. Not surprisingly, the list is as varied as it is long. She credits Claude Monet and the other Impressionists as her biggest inspiration. Vincent van Gogh's use of raw color, Henri Matisse's undulating paper cutout forms, Georgia O'Keefe's sensuous flowers, the Japanese woodblock prints of Hokusai and the Edo period all impress her with their beauty and relationships to the natural world. In our modern era, the sculptor, photographer and environmentalist Andy Goldsworthy's landscape art resonates with her. Among her mentors, she credits textile artists Sister Mary Remy Revor, and Lenore Davis at the Arrowmont School of Arts and Crafts—part of the University of Tennessee—as well as her father and brother, both pilots. Of her brother, she says, "We are a well-oiled team."

Of course, I am interested in the professional artist as a woman. Mary Edna, unlike many women artists, has been extremely successful. Perhaps it is her independence or that her vision is in synch with today's concerns about changes in our planet, with our modern awareness of our place in the universe and our fascination with the newest frontiers of exploration. I see that she is passionate about her work and her mission. Yet she conveys her message with skillful beauty and genteel charm.

When I was an art student, one of my teachers gave an apt definition of memorable artists. First, there are the Innovators. They are the ones who create perspectives and techniques that are totally new. Then there are the Classicists. They rely on the forms and methods of others that have proven the test of time. And then there are the Masters. They combine the best of the tried-and-true with innovation. Mary Edna Fraser fits the description, and her work is truly memorable.

Intrigued by Mary Edna's scientific background, I was prompted to explore her Renaissance-like ability to combine logic with artistic insight. How would she recommend that artists go about developing their own scientific skills?"

She replied that she was blessed with very good math and language skills, that her father and brother, as engineers, helped her develop both sides of her brain. She believes you always cultivate what you're interested in. She'd tell artists to find a subject they're sincerely passionate about, then to go find out all they can about it and find the scientists who can help them.

Mary Edna is passionate about the potential catastrophic changes facing our world. She possesses the knowledge and truth that science brings to us. She uses the beauty of her world vision to punctuate what damage we have already done, to inspire us to preserve what we have, and to appreciate the poetry of what nature builds and destroys.

I ask her which person—living or dead—would she most want to own some of her work. Without hesitation, she replies, "Amelia Earhart." I should have known. These are two women who share a kindred spirit. Amelia soared in the most advanced airplanes of her day to break aviation records. Today we soar with Mary Edna on wings of silk, dye, and wax.

Photo: Cathleen O'Brien

Carriage Horse

Kathy China

DAN. Even the name sounded steady and dependable. He, the beautiful Belgian steed who had never frightened a single tourist, trod the streets of downtown Charleston. The sturdy clop of his hooves accompanied the narrative of the tour guide, creating a tempo that lulled the carriage passengers into sublime relaxation.

"Here, on the Battery, is where the first shots of the Civil War were fired," explained the female tour guide dressed in a uniform inspired by the Confederacy. The carriage moved along cobblestone streets. It was a balmy June day. The breeze lifted Dan's forelock gently, while Sunny, his harnessed Belgian partner, blew through his nostrils.

Dan and Sunny easily pulled the 1200-pound black carriage with the twelve tourists and tour operator back to 50 Anson Street, where the carriage horses were stabled and cared for. The horses had stopped automatically at key attractions on the fifty-minute tour, and wended their way through vehicular and pedestrian traffic.

Dan's ears moved forward expectantly when they reached the barn on Anson Street. Soon the water misters sprayed a cool mist on the Belgians' dark orange coats. The team stopped at the water trough, and a sixteen-year-old groom, Amy, caught Dan's harness. There were slurping sounds as both horses gulped the fresh water.

"Easy, pretty boy." Amy touched Dan's rump, then lifted his tail to place the thermometer. "Very good," she soothed as she looked at the numbers. Sunny was next.

"I bet you're wishing you were back on John's Island on winter vacation," Amy said, referring to the three months Dan and Sunny had been out to pasture and allowed to kick, rear, and nip each other. "Those three months had you all fat and sassy. Now you're working for your food again."

Bobby Anders, the manager who stood nearby with several other grooms, interjected, "But I don't miss the high vet bills caused by their shenanigans." The $60,000

- $80,000 annual budget allocated for veterinary care was exceeded when the horses were injured due to unfettered rough play. Sylvia looked around at the grooms. "By the way, I will be here tomorrow before the tours start to complete the horses' monthly exams," he announced. "You'll need to be here at four-thirty instead of five in the morning to start taking and logging the temperatures. After you feed the horses and check their water, one of you will assist Sylvia, while the others start grooming, washing, and medicating each horse as the medical exam is completed."

"Will we still be ready for the nine o'clock tours?" Amy asked.

"Yes. You have a full crew of good workers coming in the morning. If you don't get the stalls stripped and new shavings added before harnessing you can do it after the carriages leave."

Another groom stepped up to help Amy unfasten the diaper from the rigging that held it in place at Dan's backside. They moved in unison to dump it before reattaching it and moving on to Sunny.

As she worked, Amy called over her shoulder to her boss, "When do I get the boom truck? The manure dumpster is getting full."

"I'm bringing it over from the shop today," Bobby replied. "Tomorrow night, I'll rotate these horses. Sylvia is going to the other barn to vet the horses before they get here."

"OK. Here we go, boys," Amy said. "Let's get you loaded." The second tour was about to begin.

Tours completed, Dan and Sunny settled into their stalls for evening rations. It was a familiar routine for the horses. The caretakers watched closely for any sign of colic or distress. The grooms kept them watered, fed, washed, and groomed. The salt of their sweat had no time to damage their sleek coats, which were monitored closely for any signs of rubbing from their harnesses.

The second shift had ended and only two staff members, known as barn girls, remained when a female figure began to pace restlessly along the walkway on the second floor of the stable. She began raising and lowering the small lift impatiently.

"D-d-did you see that?" one barn girl asked the other while pointing to the second floor.

"Yes," the girl whispered. "Let's get out of here. This place gives me the creeps late at night."

"I mean, did you see the . . . the ghost? She looks like a little girl wearing a white dress. And the lift, the lift was moving up and down."

"It's late. My tired eyes can see movement almost anywhere. Let's just get out of here."

"Yeah, I guess you're right. I'm tired."

The two made their way to the door, securing the last pitchforks on their wall hooks and switching off the lights before exiting the building.

I thought they would never leave, Mary, the ghostly figure, thought. Now downstairs, Mary moved from stall to stall, in search of a horse to mount. She selected one of the animals, a handsome Percheron. Her toes found the narrow slits between stall boards as she carefully worked her way to the top of the partition. From there, she could surely get astride the tall, broad animal. But as she reached the top boards, the horse startled and jumped over the stall door. Mary wailed in frustration.

Dan's head jerked up with his ears pointed. The bolting Percheron stopped in front of Dan's stall. Dan touched noses with him and sniffed. Unharmed, but frightened, the Percheron remained close to Dan's side. Calmed, he stared back at his stall. Dan stared too. Nothing.

Mary, now invisible, had sunk into the stall shavings. She knew she didn't have many options. Without the assistance of others, she would not be able to mount a horse. She quietly made her way back up the stairs, careful not to disturb the horses again. She loved horses with all her might. She had waited so long to ride again, since that day when she was six . . . since the deadly accident. *Tomorrow. Tomorrow, during the vet's visit. That is my only chance,* thought Mary.

The following morning Bobby checked on the grooms and veterinarian before he set off to meet the farrier at a nearby café. After managing the company for the last nine years, he was comfortable leaving the horses in the capable hands of his employees. Over coffee, the two talked about the Percheron that had been found outside his locked stall earlier that morning, with a loose shoe that needed to be reattached.

"Amy said we should call him Pegasus from now on," Bobby joked.

The farrier laughed good-naturedly. "Sounds about right to me," he said, "but you won't need my services for long if your horses take to flying."

Bobby snorted. "I hope they don't fly. That would require all new equipment, which I'm not prepared to maintain. Besides, what would become of the horse crap?" he joked.

They continued to talk about the replacement of the horses' rubber shoes and upcoming farrier work while walking back to the barn. Suddenly, a huge draft horse barreled down the street toward them. Bobby's eyes widened. "That's my horse!"

"He's spooked!" The farrier shouted and dove for a doorway.

Bobby jumped into the middle of the street and planted his feet while he waved his arms up and down in wide arcs. He'll never be able to stop. This is not going to end well, he thought.

The horse slammed to a halt in front of him. Bobby grabbed at the horse's halter and soothed him, "Easy, Dan, easy." The horse's sides heaved in and out. His eyes bulged wild with fright. "What in the world scared you, boy?"

In answer, Dan blew large droplets of snot in Bobby's face. Some things just could not be explained.

"I can't believe you jumped in front of that horse! That was either the stupidest or bravest act I have ever seen," the farrier exclaimed.

"None of this makes a bit of sense," Bobby said. "Dan is my best horse. He never startles. Never! There has to be an explanation."

Bobby walked Dan back to the stable. He met Amy halfway. Her face showed the relief she felt. "What in the world happened, Amy?"

"Sylvia had just finished examining Dan and unhooked his halter. The groom bent over to move the mounting block Sylvia used to reach his back and neck. Dan took off like someone had kicked him."

"Why would he do that? That's NOT how Dan acts."

"I don't know. Well, unless."

"Unless?"

Amy bit her lip. "Well. They claim that she probably scared the Pecheron we now call Pegasus. One of the grooms turned pale and almost passed out when she saw Dan take off."

"Ghost?" Bobby asked.

Sheepishly, Amy replied, "Yes, a ghost."

"Except there are no such things as ghosts, Amy."

Bobby led Dan into the barn. "Let's cool him down and give him the day off," he said. "We can't have any more of this nonsense."

The barn girl who was standing nearby could not contain herself. "It's that little girl ghost, Mr. Bobby. She spooked the horses."

Bobby stared at her. He opened his mouth and shut it. "I'm going to my office," he said, turning on his heel. It made no sense. Finally, he entered some key words into the search engine of his computer. The results were too broad, so he half-heartedly typed, "Girl ghost on Anson Street". The return prompt jerked him to attention.

The sad story unfolded on the screen. A six-year-old girl had met a tragic fate. In 1929, Milton Landry's carriage horses were a well-bred stock. He trained and sold the horses and drove carriages for some of Charleston's elite. Due to bad investments, Milton accumulated a good deal of debt.

One evening, he returned to the stable where two debt collectors awaited him.

As the men dragged Milton from the carriage, Milton fought fiercely, and the men fell tangled among the horse's legs. One horse pinned a brutish man with his hoof. The man removed his pistol and fired into the horse's skull.

"Noooooo!" escaped from a small girl. In a blur of motion, she attached herself to the shooter's leg. He pushed her away. She landed under the hooves of the second carriage horse, which had reared in fright. Milton Landry's six-year-old daughter, Mary, died, her lungs punctured by the hooves of the horse she loved best.

Bobby walked out of the office. It was dusk. The crew finished their last chores and he wished them good night. As he pushed the last barn door closed, the old lift creaked above his head . . . or maybe it was a moan . . . Bobby couldn't be sure. The quiet settled around him again, his spine relaxed. Then the barn door behind him blew open. He felt a sudden chill. As he spun around, he spied wispy white tendrils of mist floating out the door. *No, it couldn't be, could it?*

Mary floated through the door. *No more death.*

Dan stopped his peaceful munching. Ears erect and forward, his head lifted sharply. Dan's eyes fixed on the door, not a twitch in his entire body.

The girl was gone.

Photo: Toni Carreiro

Photo: Toni Carreiro

Folly Beach Diary

Anton DuMars

January brings quiet to Folly Beach. Distant ocean sounds and humming heat pumps provide background music to the silence. The occasional Carolina wren, cardinal, dog bark, or stray car punctuates the calm. January's salt marsh provides a different kind of quiet. Winter marsh sounds include a random dolphin breath, or maybe a red tail hawk screech, an osprey cry, a kingfisher's chatter, or an oystercatcher's whistle. Just offshore, January brings yet another quiet.

Sitting on a surfboard, isolated from land by sixty or so yards, I hear no cars or air conditioners, no wrens, or cardinals, and no kingfisher chatter—instead, I hear the periodic extended rumble of breaking waves and ripples lapping against the board.

The third week of January brings clean, long period waves. Despite an air temperature hovering just above forty, I pull on my wetsuit and paddle out alone. Gloves, booties, and suit insulate me well against winter's ocean water. A slight north wind peels the waves back a bit. Exposed ears and neck feel the wind's bite. Turbid ocean waters hide my feet.

I miss a wave and then turn to paddle back out. The lip of a breaker thumps my chest. I hear an "ugh!" and realize it is I who made that sound. A voice breaks the silence, and I realize it is me talking to myself. I talk about how cold I am. I tell myself "one wave and I'm going in." I shrug and talk to myself about talking to myself.

"People talk to themselves ..." I say. I stop talking for a while and begin listening again ... osprey, breaking waves. A peak appears on the horizon. "Here comes my wave," I say to myself. "Don't break ... hold up, wave ... come on!"

I hear vigorous paddling sounds, and then a "humph" as I spring up. Balance, look, cut ... Water rushes under the board in a "fsst, fsst" sound. Some seconds later, I dismount in the shallow white water. On my stomach, I hijack the next wave into shore. I climb from the surf and walk across the beach.

I caught my wave.

Charleston

110 Calhoun Street
Emanuel AME Church

Alphonso Brown

Manyul staat way yonduh een Fillydelpbia een sebbin teen eighty sebbin wen Richshud Allen leeh Syn Jawge Chu'ch. Dey keep on dah way 'til' dey done spread all obbuh, ebbin een Chaa'stun. Een eighteen eighteen, Moyse Brown, who bin wid Allen chu'ch, staa't tuh mek deh black people yuh fuh study deh head 'bout leebin' de white folk chu'ch. 'E pull tegedduh dem slabe, 'n free people fuh de Manyul Ch'ch wah fus'bin staa't een sebbinteen ninety one 'n staa't de new Manyul Chu'ch.

The roots of Emanuel go back to Philadelphia, where, in 1787, Richard Allen left Saint George Methodist Episcopal Church and started the African Methodist Episcopal Church. The movement spread, and in 1818, Morris Brown, an Allen supporter and a free black preacher, led the movement in Charleston to organize black Methodists into an independent organization. He reorganized the original congregation, which was started in 1791 and known as the Free African Society. It consisted of free blacks and slaves. Originally, Brown had created a circuit from the congregation of the Hampstead Church, the Anson Borough Church and the Philadelphia Alley Church in the French quarters of Charleston. In 1818, the three circuit churches were Emanuel's predecessors.

In 1834, the whites, remembering that Denmark Vesey had been a member of the original congregation, burned down the church and forbade the members to meet anymore. They met in secret until 1865, when they reorganized themselves and built a large wooden structure on the site at 110 Calhoun Street. The wooden building, which was designed by Denmark Vesey's son Robert Vesey, was destroyed in the earthquake of 1886. The current structure was completed in 1892 in its present Gothic design.

In 1882, the congregation was terribly overcrowded. To alleviate the overcrowded conditions, Emanuel bought the Zion Presbyterian building at 5 Glebe Street. Emanuel is said to be the only black church building in peninsular Charleston that was designed, built, governed and maintained by blacks. The others were donated, bought, governed or built by whites for their black congregations.

Charleston AME Church

Charleston

Sullivan's Island Bucket List

Toni Carreiro

In April 2013, I made my first visit to South Carolina with the Southern Sampler Artists Colony (SSAC). A small group of writers and artists, we were participants in a SSAC workshop, our residence was a rambling, turn-of-the-century beach house on Sullivan's Island. Shortly after arriving on the island I penned my secret South Carolina bucket list.

The first morning I headed to the beach at around 10:00 am.

The sun was bright in the Carolina sky. A California native who lives in the San Francisco Bay Area, my inner rhythm was set to Pacific Time. I was curious to learn how the Atlantic compared to the Pacific, a mighty ocean with big waves, cold water and rocky shores.

I walked across a raised wooden walkway to reach the sand dunes and beach beyond. What a surprise to see an expansive, shell-strewn beach with sandbars in the middle, and the ocean barely visible in the distance. In contrast to the Pacific, where I ran away from the waves, here I wanted to run toward them. I took off my shoes and walked along the edge of the sandbar, eager to experience the ocean close-up.

There were a few people on the beach, but I felt alone—lost in my thoughts. A long distance swimmer and tri-athlete after college, at one time I had lived to push my physical boundaries. Now a yoga enthusiast, avid dog walker and knitter, I suddenly felt an unexpected urge to dive into the seemingly calm surf that spread out as far as I could see, I wondered why I had not brought my bathing suit, whether locals swam.

Later I walked to the end of the three-mile beach, where I saw a posted sign warning people to stay out of the water because of the perilous rip tides. That's when I decided to research if, and where, it was safe to go for a dip in the waters off the island.

During the week, we enjoyed outings to downtown Charleston and areas beyond. Traveling by car from Sullivan's Island, we invariably crossed the Ravenel Bridge, a beautiful structure that spans the Cooper River and connects Charleston to Mount

Pleasant. In my mind, bridges are pathways to new adventures, and there was something especially captivating about this bridge's dramatic incline, soaring cables, and narrow pedestrian walkways. From the car window, I saw a parade of walkers and cyclists, all of whom appeared to be young and fit, moving energetically alongside the frenetic traffic.

All at once, I wanted to feel the bridge beneath my feet and get to know the Southerners using the walkways. I just had to figure out how to access the bridge.

The next time I visited South Carolina, in April 2015, again with SSAC, I had a swimsuit and walking shoes packed in my suitcase and I was determined to complete two of the challenges on my growing bucket list.

During the first writers' workshop that year, I announced to the group that I was planning to swim in the ocean and would love to have them join me. Most rolled their eyes, but a few of us set a time and day to meet. Three days later—on an overcast, windy afternoon—six of us, wearing swimsuits or shorts under our beach towels, arrived at the ocean. We shed our towels, took a deep breath, and one by one, tiptoed toward the rippling surf. Some took a quick dip and retreated to the shore. Kathy, a muscular massage therapist and yoga instructor clad in a two-piece Speedo, and I lingered in the water. I was astonished when Kathy said, "I don't know how to swim."

Thank goodness she had a floatie!

That year, I discovered, was to be the Colony's last year on Sullivan's Island because the rental property we called home was for sale. I worried that I might not return. Now was the time to walk the Ravenel Bridge. Based on my research, I knew that the bridge entry was a twelve-minute car ride from Sullivan's Island. I should park at the gas station in Mount Pleasant, located at the base of the six-mile bridge. I decided to walk half way and back, which sounded easy enough to me.

On Wednesday morning, April 22, the house was quiet. I threw on my sweats, brushed my teeth, and left before anyone could stop me. Parked at the gas station in Mount Pleasant, I tried to figure out what I should bring with me. The sun was almost overhead. I already felt the heat and humidity. No one knew where I was. *What if I have a heat stroke?* ran through my mind, followed by, *You can do this.*

Ascending the divided path—one side for cyclists and one side for walkers—I tried to appear nonchalant, but given the steep incline of the bridge, roar of traffic, and the slender guardrails, I felt dizzy. Three seniors, power-walking women, charged past me. My competitive nature propelled me forward. *If they can do it, I can do it*, became my mantra.

Once I reached the middle of the bridge, I felt jubilant. I paused to breathe in the fresh air and appreciate the spectacular view. Cargo ships passed in the water below, Fort Sumter sat on the horizon, and the Charleston harbor beckoned. I was truly grateful for my bucket list . . . for challenges and the urge to fulfill them.

I'll return to South Carolina with the SSAC this April, 2016. This time we'll be staying at Folly Beach, on the Charleston side of the Ravenel Bridge, and I'm betting that Folly, referred to by locals as "the edge of America," will inspire an entirely new bucket list.

left: The Arthur Ravenel, Jr. Bridge
right: Sullivan's Island Lighthouse
Photos: Toni Carreiro

Charleston

A southern moon is a sodden moon, and sultry. When it swamps the fields and the rustling sandy roads and the sticky honeysuckle hedges in its sweet stagnation, your fight to hold on to reality is like a protestation against a first waft of ether.

—Zelda Fitzgerald, *Save Me the Waltz*

The South

The Washboard Man   Photo: Cheryl Armstrong

Heaven Belongs to Me

Cheryl Armstrong

Heaven belongs to me... clap, clap, clap-clap-clap-clap ... *Heaven belongs to me ...*

"I'm sitting on the carpet of a terracotta-pink Charleston parlor, my Nikon in my lap. I just shot a close-up of an African American musician's brass clad fingers skipping across a nearly square washboard. His indigo trousers are anchored at his waist by a rope and his straw hat is tipped back on his head. His eyes are warm as honey and only occasionally glance my way—"Heaven belongs to me"—and in my heart I truly feel the song and the rhythm—the beat of the Christian spiritual.

I sing along, clapping my hands as he has instructed us, a roomful of "Music Café" folk, as he and his partner perform. Even her floor-length indigo Gullah dress brushes the threads of the carpet in time to the strumming and the singing ... clap, clap, clap-clap-clap-clap ... "Heaven belongs to me."

When was the last time my heart had thrummed to a beat? I remember that thirty-three years before, as a Peace Corps volunteer on my first bus ride in Ethiopia, 1972—the driver's assistant slid a tape into the machine: James Brown's "Papa's Got a Brand New Bag." Who knew that by changing continents I could grow a new ear? I heard rhythm and blues like it was for the first time. The next song that time was Brown's "Please, Please, Please."

Up next during that ride was Alemayehu Ashete, Ethiopia's own James Brown, a haunting voice with the horns of the band behind him. Though Ethiopians listened to American blues, the rock and roll and jazz brought to them via the U.S. army base radio station outside the Eritrean city of Asmara, they had music all their own—equally jazzy, even sexier and even more shake-your-booty moody. Their bands had been inspired by the unlikely source of a group of forty Armenian orphans from Jerusalem, adopted by Emperor Haile Selassie for their music. Those orphans played brass instruments and the Ethiopians of their adopted country fell in love with the sound of their brass band and incorporated it into their popular music. Ethiopian ears were ready to accept American rhythm and blues when it showed up on their radios.

The South

As for me, long before that bus ride, while still in eighth grade, I had danced to Chubby Checker: "Come on, baby, let's do the Twist." The Twist was the first American dance where you danced alone with your partner. Dancing to Chubby Checker was a revelation, a release of pre-teen sexual energy, an introduction to using my shoulders and hips to express sensuality. Chubby Checker was born in Spring Gully, South Carolina. James Brown was born in Barnwell County, South Carolina. I didn't realize it then, but I'd been listening to America's southern musicians much of my life. I'd heard Duke Ellington, Dizzy Gillespie and Louis Armstrong on my father's hi-fi.

When radio began its life in the 1920s a new kind of music found its way from New Orleans, the river towns of the American South, and African American neighborhoods in New York and Chicago to the homes of white families like my family in suburban Walnut Creek, California. Musicians like Duke Ellington and Louis Armstrong became household names. The overnight celebrities were African Americans like Ellington, Armstrong, Ella Fitzgerald, and Billie Holiday. Ellington's band performed weekly national broadcasts from the Cotton Club in Harlem. My father welcomed African American music into our living room, and my ear was trained to listen to jazz.

That summer of James Brown on the Ethiopian bus I learned to dance to Ethiopian pop music in the Ethiopian and Eritrean manner, shimmying my shoulders to Alemayehu Ashete and Mahmoud Ahmed. While I was in Peace Corps training in a town called Shashemane, we danced Friday evenings with our Ethiopian and Eritrean trainers, swapped cassette tapes and shook our hips and shoulders to African and African American music. It was a time when American pop music still had a horn section and Ethiopians loved their horns. When our trainers danced they kept their hip and foot movement to a minimum as they shimmied their shoulders.

Like African American music, Ethiopian music has its roots in liturgical sound. A large drum, a gong, a jangly metal sistrum and the pounding of prayer staffs accompany the Ethiopian church service to maintain rhythm along with chanting. It is mesmerizing. No pews in their churches, you stand and sway for many hours, as long as you can persevere in their dark incense-scented stone rooms.

My musical African American heroes grew up singing in their churches in the

South: John Coltrane, Charles Lloyd, James Brown, Nina Simone, Louis Armstrong, and on and on. Chubby Checker was even told he'd have to sing in a choir for a while when he was paroled from a Georgia jail. Then his musical career took off.

As a young girl, although I didn't know at first where they came from, I sang African American spirituals in my Presbyterian church and again as a college student as part of the folk movement: "Amazing Grace," "Go Down, Moses," "It's Me, Oh Lord," and "He's Got the Whole World in His Hands."

So my connection to the South has been through the music of African Americans from the South. I didn't know "He's Got the Whole World in His Hands" came from the South. It was just one of the songs we sang at summer camps, at anti-war demonstrations, and at Civil Rights demonstrations. In fact, it was published in a collection of spirituals as early as 1927 and collected by Frank Warner, an American folk song collector, from a singer in North Carolina in 1933.

Through my experiences with the Civil Rights movement, I woke up, and the lyrics themselves taught me. And now, when I think of gospel songs and spirituals I know them as southern songs that most often originated among enslaved Africans in southern states, sung while they worked and when they attended church. Many spirituals have been sung since the 1600s.

Even Nina Simone's "Sinner Man" is accepted as an African American traditional spiritual song. Nina Simone was the sixth child of a preacher's family in North Carolina. A famous rendition of "Nobody Knows the Trouble I've Seen" was done by Louis Armstrong, the man who trained my ear in my living room. I can hear his raspy voice: "Nobody knows the trouble I've seen, glory hallelujah."

From liturgical music and spirituals, to pop music and jazz, to rhythm and blues and rock and roll, from dancing and losing yourself to the beat, to cross cultural sharing of sound and senses—music is really quite remarkable and human, and for me it is rooted in America's South and the Ethiopian beat.

At that Music Café in that lovely Charleston home, I have a conversation with a Charlestonian about music in the South. "Music is different in the various states here in the South," she insists, "South Carolina from Louisiana from Tennessee."

The South

Louisiana gave us Louis Armstrong, the grandson of slaves. Alabama gave us Percy Sledge ("When a Man Loves a Woman") and Martha Reeves of Martha and the Vandellas ("Dancing in the Street", a 1964 Motown hit). B. B. King, the son of sharecroppers, was born on a cotton plantation in Mississippi. T-Bone Walker, of African American and Cherokee descent and acclaimed American blues guitarist, was born in Linden, Texas. Two more of my favorite jazz musicians, Thelonius Monk and John Coltrane, were born in North Carolina. Tina Turner was born in Nutbush, Tennessee. Her song "What's Love Got to Do With It?" helped me through my divorce.

When I return to California from my trip to Charleston, I attend a jazz concert in San Francisco. Charles Lloyd headlines. Lloyd grew up in Memphis, Tennessee. His roots are African, Cherokee, Mongolian, and Irish. He was exposed to different music than James Brown and Chubby Checker—to Memphis's river culture—but also, like them, to blues, gospel and jazz. That night at the jazz club he performs "All My Trials"—not exactly a gospel song, but deeply spiritual.

Finally there is a white boy's song about the South. When he sings, "In my mind I'm goin' to Carolina . . ." it means something to me, because now I've been to South Carolina four times and I love being reminded of the place. "Can't you just feel the sunshine? Can't you just feel the moonshine? Ain't it just like a friend of mine, to hit me from behind?" Simple lyrics, maybe, but when I hear it, I'm there.

The same is true when I hear Alemayu Ashete. I want to go back to Ethiopia. And James Brown, well, he takes me back to my youth. And Nina Simone, she takes me to my soul. Where would my spirit be without my southern musicians?

The Washboard Man and The Gullah Lady Photo: Cheryl Armstrong

The South

What Remains

The grandfather I never knew

drowned July 4th, 1935,

but not before he saved

his four children and wife,

When a sudden storm capsized his sailboat

they held fast to the boom.

Granddad's remains were found days later.

My mother,

five years old at the time,

remembered his drowning sobs:

"See you in Glory."

A porcelain urn depicts

mood of the raging storm that took him

far away . . .

symbolically holds the memory of his ashes

that rode the waves and found home shore

in West Africa

—*Ty Collins*

Urn with a Legend
Pastel on parchment
Ty Collins

Washing Ashore
Water-based oil on
canvas board
Ty Collins

The South

Pen and Ink Drawing. Fishbone Tree
After Hurricane Hugo came through Bishopville in 1989,
Pearl planted this Leyland Cypress. It took seven years to grow
the tree into a design often described as a "fishbone".

—*Cathleen O'Brien*

Pearl Fryar's Garden

Martha Dabbs Greenway

The first time I visited Pearl Fryar's garden is a story in itself. It was in early spring when my friend Myra and I decided to drive the twenty-five miles from Sumter, South Carolina, over to Bishopville. I wanted to find this fabulous topiary garden I had read about so when we got to Bishopville, she pulled into the Exxon station to ask directions.

"Excuse me," I yelled out the window to the man pumping gas. "Do you know how I'd find Pearl Fryar's garden?"

"Yes, ma'am, I do," he said with a smile. "He's my neighbor."

Bishopville's population is under 4,000, but even I didn't expect the man putting gas into his car to be Pearl Fryar's neighbor! We easily found the incredible topiary garden on Broad Acres Road and, yes, it is fabulous, but we will get to that story in a moment. As we were leaving town, I spotted a van literally covered in cameras, parked beside the Welcome to Bishopville sign. Excited, I asked Myra to pull over. I hopped out and approached the young driver of the van.

"Y'all not from around here, are you?" I asked.

"No, we're from California." He introduced himself as Harrod Blank, a filmmaker and photographer from Berkeley. "We're here to film the Button Man."

I had met Dalton Stevens, known locally as the Button King, at the Sumter County Fair. Legend has it Dalton couldn't sleep one night so he decided to sew some buttons onto his clothes. Before he knew it, he had completely covered his jacket, trousers, and hat with buttons, and went on to cover a coffin, a Chevrolet Chevette and even a toilet with buttons as well.

"Well, you also need to talk to Pearl Fryar, the Plant Man," I said. The Camera Van, the Button King, the Plant Man—all in one afternoon in Bishopville. The Button King showed up in Blank's film, *Automorphosis*; I showed up in Pearl Fryar's garden dozens more times, often with Southern Sampler friends in tow.

The South

The first time I remember actually meeting Pearl was the winter of 2002. I worked for the Sumter County Cultural Commission and we were sponsoring a visual arts exhibition called *Out of Necessity: Art Driven by the Soul*. It featured paintings and sculptures created by artists using "the means available" to communicate and express feelings, dreams, and concepts. In Pearl's case it meant creating a magical topiary garden with shrubs discarded by the local plant nursery. His mathematical mind led him to trim those plants to within an inch of their life into geometric shapes— beautiful squares, boxes, triangles and pyramids.

Pearl didn't stop with discarded greenery. He also created pieces of sculpture from bits and pieces of found metal objects, clay pots, or used printing plates from the soft drink canning company where he worked. One of the sculptures he brought for the exhibit had the words "Love and Unity" on one side and "Hate Hurts" on the other. I would learn through the years that this man who carved out "Love, Peace and Goodwill" in the grassy part of his garden really lived those philosophies.

A couple of years later during the Cultural Commission's installation art exhibition called "Accessibility," Pearl worked with hundreds of high school students to create a mosaic garden in a vacant space off Main Street in Sumter. For several years he was artist-in-residence with the art department of Coker College in nearby Hartsville. One of his large topiaries was transplanted to the grounds of the South Carolina State Museum in Columbia and smaller pieces of his sculpture are in their collection. Nationally and internationally known in gardening circles, he is a sought-after public speaker.

Pearl once told me that he didn't know he was an artist until we invited him to be a part of *Out of Necessity* and told him he was one. Here is a man who could see fountains and sculptures in materials most people would discard and create amazing shapes out of shrubs and trees left to die and rarely, if ever, used in topiary. It's a good thing somebody told him that what he was doing was art.

Photo: Maureen Dixon

Three Poems

William Harrison (Billy) Vandiver

GREEN TEA

Rainbows, ruby tucked
Rabbits' noses, perking up
Syncopated, wonder struck

Hallucinations etched in rhymes
Painted buntings on the vines
Mother-of-pearls from golden times
Peacocks nesting in a line

Ruddy twinkles
Packed in petals
'Cause there's stash not steam
In Grandma's kettle

PICKLES

Preen a peck of pickles
'til they are just right
the moon glow on their waxy skins
pleasing guests all night

the sour,
the dill,
the evening's chill

cures an ailing pucker
with a kosher thrill

SOUL FOOD

Sublime temptations
wrestle in my heart
to rhyme in real time
with my soul's guitar

A Jewish Girl Considers Conversion

Bring on the barbeque
Soft shell crab and mush—
I'm starting to turn Southern,
So sit right down and hush.

Deviled eggs and cornbread,
Crawdads and their kids.
I'll pull some pork and shell some shrimp—
All food my faith forbids.

There'll be collard greens and okra—
Hold the bagels, no more lox—
When I start to chomp on chitlin's,
Oy, my kosher friends will *plotz!*

I won't forget the spirits—
I'll pour bourbon and sweet tea.
If I build a porch and get some chairs
You all can rock with me.

We'll share carrot cake and pralines,
Peach ice cream and shoofly pie.
In a short time Jew and Gentile
Will be One under the sky.

— Nancy Alpert

Smells and Spice and Everything Nice

Cheryl Armstrong

Did you know black pepper comes in different flavors?

I'm eight-years-old standing in Doris' kitchen doorway, hoping she'll invite me to dinner. My friend, Janice, is still in her room with her dolls, and I've had enough of that.

I desire Janice's Mom's plump green lima beans with juicy smoked ham hocks, sautéed golden onions and garlic and black pepper. If Doris invites me to dinner, I'll shake on extra black pepper, bite into the lima beans, and suck the meat off the bone. Doris hasn't made her biscuits yet. I want to watch her measure the powdery flour, cut in the butter, pour the milk, and work the dough. On the stove is a pot of greens, simmering with more sautéed onions.

"Darlin', it's near time for you to head home. Your Momma must be blowin' her whistle."

I frown. I haven't heard the whistle, the one my mother uses to fetch my brother. Maybe I have more time. I stall because at my house there will be plain boiled potatoes and roasted or fried meat with frozen green beans. My mother will say, "Add your own salt." She is Vermont born, transplanted to California.

Doris is Maryland born, cooks southern style and has a spice cabinet full of the most wonderful colors and smells. Her lobster bisque practically makes my Daddy cry into his holiday cocktail every Christmas. Her southern cooking changed my life.

Fourteen years later Doris gives me a going away party when I join the Peace Corps to head off to Ethiopia. She offers me a big bowl of her spicy crab dip. "I've heard Ethiopian cuisine will challenge your palate, honey. Try this; it's hot."

Doris' dip is spicy and delicious with paprika and tobasco sauce. But it does not challenge my palate the way berbere does in Ethiopia. Traditionally berbere is made up of hot red peppers dried on straw mats in the sun, pounded in a wooden mortar, then mixed with herbs, spices, dried onions, garlic and salt. Another important Ethiopian spice is mitmita. Orange-red in color, it contains ground bird's eye chili peppers (piri piri), cardamom seed, cloves and salt. Sometimes it has cinnamon, cumin and ginger in it.

I meet these spices in a buna bet in Shashemane, my training town, south of Addis Ababa. Tsegaye and Berhane, two of my Peace Corps trainers, bring me and a few fellow volunteers for our first injera and wat to what they hope will be the mildest introduction to Ethiopian cuisine: aliche and kai wat ordered special for farengis (foreigners.) Injera is a whitish grey round spongy sourdough flatbread made from teff, an Ethiopian grain. Wat is Ethiopian stew served on the injera which is spread on a tray, like a food towel.

Following a demonstration, I tear off a strip of injera and use it to pick up a chunk of spiced meat and pop the package in my mouth. Wowie kazowie, is it hot! It is hotter than Mexican chili peppers; hotter than Indian spices; and definitely hotter than Doris' crab dip.

Some injera is dark, some light. Just like biscuits, there's good injera and injera that's not so good. Traditional injera is made over charcoal fire. In fact, the closest I've ever come to these Ethiopian dishes is Doris' cooking. An equivalent to Doris' lima beans would be the mesir wat or kik aliche which are the split red lentils in berbere sauce or split pea stew in turmeric sauce. An equivalent to Doris' greens would be gomen, collard greens cooked with onions.

At the next table at that buna bet an Ethiopian gentleman dips two-inch cubes of raw beef into a bowl of berbere powder and pops them into his mouth as if they are as bland as flour. "He thinks the berbere will kill the tapeworm," Tsegaye says. "Eventually he'll get an ulcer. We all get stomach ulcers from raw meat and berbere."

I grow to love Ethiopian cuisine as much as I love Doris' cooking: Doro wat (spicy hot chicken stew), yebeg wat (lamb stew), awaze tibs (cubed lamb with ginger and onions and many spices), yetsom beyaynetu (a vegetarian platter of shiro, or chickpeas, and other vegetables), and injera.

After Ethiopia I live in Turkey and the Pacific Northwest and travel to Southeast

Asia, Bali, Indonesia, New Zealand and much of Europe. Everywhere I go there is a spice market and a new cuisine to try. Every spring I visit South Carolina and enjoy shrimp cooked with bacon and onions and black pepper. Oh, my—black pepper.

Black peppercorns come from India, Indonesia, Vietnam, Malaysia, and Brazil. They vary in acidity and sweetness and can be more or less aromatic and citrusy. In my spice cupboard in addition to berbere I store spices from all over the world and five different black peppers. While in Charleston I buy myself two big bags of grits, a box of Blazin Blends, Zesty Seasoned Salt, and a box of Old Bay Seasoning a piquant mixture of celery seed, salt, red pepper, black pepper, and paprika used in Frogmore stew, crab cakes, deviled eggs, soups, stews, gumbo and other Lowcountry boils.

I love it when my grown son Nuri, born in Istanbul, now living in the East Bay, stops by for a visit. He opens the spice cabinet and says, "I know I'm in Mom's home when I open this cupboard. Sweet smells."

Mami Wata

*(For Cookie Washington, who hears the call
of the Black Mermaid Goddess)*

can't wait

don't wana wait

tired of waiting

wanna jump in

swim

like Mami Wata

become

Deity

of your African waters

wanna

become one

with moon

sun

sky

grasp the shore of your existence

and pull you in

—Joanna Crowell

Black Mermaids

Cindy Rasicot

It's hard to believe that Torreah "Cookie" Washington's passionate interest in the black mermaids and powerful goddesses of the sea was sparked by a children's book. In 2001, she discovered *Her Stories: African American Folktales, Fairy Tales and True Tales*, written by Newbury Medalist, Virginia Hamilton.

One story in particular, "Mary Belle and the Mermaid", captured Cookie's imagination and inspired her to search for more information about black mermaids and merwomen. According to Cookie, that story gave birth to the Fiber Arts Exhibit: *Mermaids and Merwomen in Black Folklore*. Curated by Cookie, the 2012 exhibit opened at the City Gallery, located at Waterfront Park Charleston, South Carolina, and featured the largest collection of mermaid-themed quilts and dolls ever exhibited.

As a resident of the San Francisco Bay Area, I knew about Cookie's interest in black goddesses prior to meeting her. Each spring I attend the Southern Sampler Artists Colony Writers retreat held in the South Carolina Lowcountry. Cookie had suggested that the Bay Area workshop participants visit the Room of the Dons at the Mark Hopkins, a landmark hotel located on Nob Hill, San Francisco. There, mounted on the wall, is a picture of Queen Calafia, a fictional Amazon warrior who lived and ruled over a kingdom of black women on the mythical island of California. Calafia has been depicted as the spirit of California.

Intrigued by the myths of black goddesses, I decided to call Cookie and ask for an interview. I phoned her, as fate would have it, soon after several writers attending a 2015 retreat dared one another to go swimming in the ocean—in spite of the brisk April wind and cold water.

The subject of the swim came up in our conversation. Cookie's voice deepened. "If you're going to go swimming, before you get into the water say a prayer for all the black souls of the slaves who were delivered on that shore on their passage from Africa."

A chill went up my spine at the thought of our proposed swim. It hadn't occurred to me that the *water* would be filled with the spirits of enslaved Africans.

The South

I could hardly wait to interview Cookie.

She chose to meet at a Japanese restaurant in Charleston. Seated in a booth, I glanced out a nearby window and watched Cookie park her car. She was talking on her cell phone, and I got the impression that she was a busy person flying from one appointment to the next. A short, husky black woman wearing a floor-length black caftan with splashes of white and crimson, Cookie approached the entrance with a confident stride. Her eyes brightened as she slid into the booth, apparently delighted to talk about one of her favorite subjects: black female goddesses.

We began with the exhibit she curated in 2012. "We had 110 pieces in the City Gallery at Waterfront Park—the largest exhibit they had ever had," she said. "I told someone if I had died the night of my opening, I'd have died the happiest woman in the world."

Curious, I asked Cookie to tell me more about her interest in black mermaids and the origins of the exhibit.

"The year before the exhibit, on Halloween, I saw four little black girls dressed as 'Ariel' from Disney's *Little Mermaid*," she said. "You know Ariel—pale white skin with red hair. I reflected on how sad this was that these little girls probably only know a watered down story of the mermaid myth. I wanted little girls, like my friend Asia Rose, to know that mermaids are not just the stuff that Disney movies are made of.

"Mermaids are goddesses, supernatural beings that were worshiped by many tribes and people along the West Coast of Africa. Yemaya is a West African creation goddess, often depicted as a mermaid. The legend states that Yemaya's womb spilled forth the fourteen Yoruba goddesses and gods, and the breaking of her uterine waters caused a great flood, which created the oceans."

I had never heard of the Yoruba people, an ethnic group from southwestern Nigeria and southern Benin in West Africa. Yoruba territory was known as the Slave Coast and many of the slaves brought to Charleston were direct descendants of the Yoruba people.

Cookie continued to talk about Yemaya. "She birthed the first human woman and man, who became the parents of all mortal beings on earth. Ever since the time black slaves first arrived in the South Carolina Lowcountry in 1670, they brought with them the stories of the ocean and river goddesses. They carried the stories in their hearts and heads."

There is no written documentation of these mermaid stories because black slaves were forbidden to learn to read or write under penalty of death, and in many cases they were forced to abandon the spiritual practices of their homeland and embrace the faith of their masters.

Cookie leaned forward, determination in her voice. "I want all little girls and my daughters to know that black women were not just slaves, domestics and entertainers, but that we were Amazon goddesses, queens, great warriors, brilliant medicine women and we can go on to become astronauts, pilots and marine biologists, heart surgeons and brain surgeons and, yes, even President of the United States."

I leaned toward Cookie, concentrating on her passionate message.

"You don't know about the richness of black women in America or around the world," she said with resigned conviction. "I was so surprised to discover women who looked like me—who were black or fat—were worshipped as Goddesses. How empowering is that? How much does that change the way that you look at yourself? That is why this was important to me."

Cookie picked up a five-by-seven card from her purse and handed it to me. It was a photograph of a dark underwater scene depicting a black mermaid swimming with sea creatures and surrounded by silhouettes of black human beings holding spears. The words on the card read, "The water brought us, the water will take us home."

Cookie's face became somber as she explained that the card was a photograph of an extraordinary quilt by Laura Gadson dedicated to the incident at Ibo Landing. She spoke slowly. "In 1803, seventy-five slaves got off of the boat at Ibo Landing in Georgia. These people, who were chained together—mothers, fathers, children—saw the other enslaved ones on the shore, and they saw them being beaten. They all held hands and walked backwards into the sea and drowned themselves." Cookie wiped away the tear sliding down her cheek.

"They did that because they believed that the mermaid would take their souls

The South

back to the motherland and on to heaven. There is a Negro spiritual called "Freedom" and the line goes, 'Before I'll be a slave, I'll be buried in my grave.' That song came from the incident at Ibo Landing. These people were so strong. They were willing to die in order not to be enslaved."

I pushed the thought of swimming in the Atlantic from my mind and attempted to lighten the moment. I asked Cookie if she had a favorite mermaid story.

Cookie was quick to respond. "A man, who looked like an old raisin, came to the City Gallery exhibit. When nearly everyone had left, he came up to me. 'Come sit with me,' he said, pointing to two nearby chairs. 'I'm going to tell you a mermaid story.

"'I have been a fisherman since I was four-years-old,' the withered man began. 'My daddy and my uncle would go out to sea, and we'd catch our fish, our crabs, and our shrimp. But sometimes they'd catch a big fish and they would cut off its head and they'd only bring the bottom part of the fish back, and it was a mermaid.'

"That's what he told me," said Cookie. "I thought that was the coolest thing that he had this story. People say, 'oh, they mistake mermaids for manatees,' but I don't think so. Christopher Columbus saw mermaids. He said that they were not as attractive as he thought they might be and I thought, *You are not that attractive either.*"

Cookie smiled when I ask her how she defined the divine feminine.

"What a great question," she exclaimed. "Thank you. I define the divine feminine as our deepest, innermost spiritual power and our magic and wisdom. I think the seat of everybody's wisdom is based in the feminine. If you meet a wise man like the Dalai Lama, his wisdom is very feminine. It's very gentle, but strong. I think this new Pope is in touch with the divine feminine. The seat of our power is the divine feminine, and it's a place we should all strive to get to."

We had been talking for ninety minutes. My attention was beginning to fade, but without a doubt, Cookie could have gone on and on.

As for that upcoming swim, I resolved to lead the writers in prayer before we entered the water.

Mural of Queen Calafia in the Room of the Dons at the Mark Hopkins Hotel, San Francisco, California

The South

Pawleys Island Cottages

paintings by Ann Langston

In September 1989, Hurricane Hugo plowed through Pawleys Island, South Carolina, smashing cottages that had for a century defined the essence of that community. After the storm, some cottages were missing while others lay damaged beyond repair. I was saddened to find that large homes were being built on lots where two or three cottages had once stood.

That's when I began painting images of the remaining cottages. I wanted to preserve them, especially for myself. My love affair with the island continues after fifty years of visiting Pawleys. I spend time there with my family and friends every April, and carry that love of "my island" in my heart all through the year.

—Ann Langston

The South

You Are as Young as the Sun

You are as young as the sun, which has yet to rise on a new day

You are as beautiful as the flower that sleeps within its bud until the bloom of day

You are the answer to the question that has not been asked

You are God's promises fulfilled

His dreams come to pass

In one holy creature vastly conceived in pure Light

You are the dream of all tomorrow's possibilities

You are the cystalline perception of His Holy Grace

You are everything, nothing more than every man's potential

You are so much more than Earthly eyes perceive

For you are yesterday's regrets translated into tomorrow's hopes

You are fine and polished with a luminous glow

A Light that guides you home to the tomorrow of hopes fulfilled

Promises kept—all debts prepaid

You are fully grown in Love's Light and protection

Grown to full measure of your heavenly height

Grown, matured, and ready to blossom

Into a new day dawning

Where Light shines on everyone the same

Where hope becomes reality, and ceases to be dreamed about

Where higher and higher we rise

To greet each other eye to eye

And see for the first time

Our commonality

Our Oneness

Our salvation

From separation and longing

Our yearning days departed

Our hopelessness left behind

Joy in the morning

Joy will greet the New Day dawning

On Earth returned to paradise

You, you are the seedling of this new territory

You hold the hope of the world in your heart

Planted there long ago by God

To be fertilized

Nourished and unearthed

For all to see

You, growing into the hope of tomorrow

The South

You, rising from within your core

To heights above the common man

To explore the New World dawning

Explore you will

Then travel back

Show the Way to others

Till all arrive

On the shore

Of the New Day's dawning

The Sun will rise on that new day

The darkness disappearing

The hope

The peace

The love abounding

Ever lasting

Amen

—*Kathie Corley/Cerantha*

Photo: Mary Jean (MJ) Pramik

The South

The Two Winter Coats

William Alexander (Billy) Dabbs

Mama Sadie wore her winter coat to the women's church circle meeting during the late spring. A few women put their coats in the bedroom of the hostess. The weather was so nice that it was not necessary to put the coats on when they left the house.

That fall, when cool weather began to settle in, Mama Sadie's coat was much too long. Without thinking, she had the coat shortened to fit. Within a few weeks, Mrs. Newman came by to show Mama Sadie the short coat she had and wondered if there could have been a mix-up. Both realized where and when the error was made. Mrs. Newman was without funds to purchase another coat, so she had to shorten the coat even more to make it into a jacket.

Coldstream Gardens

William Alexander (Billy) Dabbs

Miss Hammie had one of the most beautiful gardens in the South. The gardens were within sight of the church. Miss Hammie rented her plantation to J. F. Bland Sr. for cash rent in advance of the crop year. Very few farmers could muster that much money and most rent was paid with a share of the crops or in cash after the frost. Miss Hammie wanted to travel to Europe to see the great gardens over there. She borrowed the money from Bland with the agreement that he could buy the farm at a certain price if she died within five years. She died within that time and Bland changed the gardens to a cotton field. Many of the plants and shrubs were sold to Fruitland Nurseries in Augusta Georgia, and many of these plants can be seen today at the Master's Golf Club. The travel money was still in the bank at her death.

Series of Errors

William Alexander (Billy) Dabbs

I toy with things and ideas that I cannot master. The desire to write with proper spelling and grammar is not my forté. One theory is that what can't be done right should not be done at all. My idea is that errors are better than nothing at all, even when errors have disastrous effects. My son, Bill, said that the inscription on my tombstone should be "Here lies a series of errors," and I replied, "You might be one."

The Bottle Tree

(Novel Excerpt)

Mary Brent Cantarutti

There was a gentle breeze when they set out for the island: Charlie in the front of the canoe, Lou in the back, and a mutt named Hunter curled up in the middle.

"It's a beautiful morning," Lou said, looking up at the puffs of white clouds nestled in the blue South Carolina sky. "You always knew what to do with a paddle, Charlie. Think I'll leave it up to you." She placed the paddle across her knee.

He looked at her, momentarily letting the canoe drift. "From now on we're sharing the same canoe and we both paddle. Remember how we liked to time ourselves, see how quickly we could paddle out to the island?" he asked. "I seem to recall our best time was about fifteen minutes. Think we can beat that record?"

"I can't believe you are suggesting a race to the island, Charlie." Lou batted her eyes. "Aren't you plumb worn out after last night?"

"I've never felt better in my life," he quipped. "It's the kind of work that agrees with me. And how about you, my dear? Are you up to racing after last night?" He relished the playful intimacy.

"You bet."

He liked that about her, the way she was always game for a challenge.

"Let's go," she said.

The paddles dipped into the still water like synchronized knives cutting soft butter. Faster and faster they glided over the bay, picking up an easy, shared rhythm as they approached the island lined by a ribbon of green trees. Charlie tightened his grip on the paddle. Just tell her; just tell her ran through his mind, a dread that had caught fire.

"We need to finalize a plan to prevent toxic waste disposal in Clarksville, Lou-

Du." He fought to keep his voice even, but he could feel swirls of grey mist enveloping his heart—the same heart that might stop beating at any moment; the heart he had lost to Lou.

"Why do I get the feeling that you haven't told me everything?" she asked. Lou leaned into the paddle.

Charlie matched her stroke for stroke. "Let's concentrate on beating that fifteen-minute record," he replied. "We can rest and talk at the Resurrection Tree."

How many times had she heard Charlie tell the story about the Resurrection Tree? It was a story told to him by his Grandfather DuBose—a story about a noble cypress cut down in the 1930s when 170,000 acres of swamp and timberland was cleared to make way for a dam, manmade lakes, and a hydroelectric plant. It was a story with a happy ending. The tree that had been sacrificed to create light, as well as DuBose Bay, had grown back to emerge triumphantly from its dark, watery grave. Lou and Charlie had often sought a little shade under its lacy leaves. Once they had looked up to discover a huge water moccasin coiled around a branch. That was the only time Lou recalled Charlie wishing that he had a gun. Today there were no snakes to be seen; only a single white egret. It took flight the moment Lou and Charlie brought the canoe to rest under the tree.

"So what's going on with toxic waste disposal in Clarksville, Charlie?" Lou skipped over small talk, leaned back, and crossed her arms.

He let out a sigh of relief, grateful for her directness. He turned on the seat to face her. "There's a County Council meeting tomorrow night," he said matter-of-factly. "There'll be a motion to rezone the DuPree land from agriculture to business. Earth-star wants to lease the land for toxic waste disposal."

Lou's stomach clutched. She felt choked by betrayal. The DuPree land was her father's sacred legacy. As a child, she had often heard him say: "The land gives to those who plant the seeds, tend the crops, and harvest to plant again." Now, seated on the bench in the back of the canoe, she could almost feel the DuPree's sandy, porous soil, sifting through her fingers.

"How do we stop them?" Lou asked, looking Charlie squarely in the eye.

The South

"Well, I have a few hunters lined up to defend the environment and local wild-life," he replied.

"I hope they arrive at the meeting in their trucks with gun racks loaded and growling dogs in those traveling pens," Lou said.

"We have a lot of ground to cover between now and tomorrow night," Charlie acknowledged. He took in the sight of Lou wearing her skimpy shorts and halter-top. He didn't want to go anywhere, except maybe to bed.

"Okay, but let's get one thing straight, Charlie." Lou glanced at the spreading branches of the Resurrection Tree, seeking reassurance. Slowly she stood, and gingerly made her way to the front of the canoe. "Move over, Hunter," she ordered. "I'm claiming a different space."

Lou settled herself in Charlie's lap despite Hunter's jealous growling. "You're my one and only knight, Charlie. I have loved you. I love you. I'll always love you."

Now she had said it all. A sprinkling of cleansing tears trickled down her cheeks.

"I love you, too, Lou-Du, with all my heart." He paused, taking in the sweet smell of her. "You mean everything to me, Lou-Du." He lifted the gold heart from her chest, brushed it across his lips. "I don't know what's going to happen, but I'd be a happy man if I died right here, with you in my lap and Hunter underfoot."

She held on to him with all her might. She didn't want to think about ever losing Charlie. "Can we save the DuPree land and DuBose Bay?" she asked.

It was a question that couldn't be answered with a simple "yes" or "no." Charlie ran his long fingers through Lou's wild curls and considered the best response. Slowly he lifted her face, brushed his lips against hers.

"Together, we're going to fight for what we believe in, and what we've been given. We're going to be sure that sacred places like DuBose Bay are here when we are gone— that there's an island for the geese to come to in the fall, a place for the purple martins to come to in the spring, and a place for our spirits ... our souls ... to call home."

"Oh, Charlie, you've done it again; made me smile when I wanted to cry." Lou could have been Cinderella. The shoe finally fit. She had found her true love—only to have a wicked fate threaten to steal her magic shoe. She carefully unfolded herself from Charlie's tender embrace. "Dare you to go skinny dipping," she said, determined to break a bad spell. She stood, twirled her hips, and puckered her lips, all the time praying that the canoe wouldn't capsize. "We could have a lot of fun," she teased, sliding the waistband of her shorts down an inch or two.

Charlie let out a playful roar. "Come to me, my cupcake queen." He stretched out his arms. The canoe rocked dangerously. Now they both laughed. "Wish I could join you, Lou-Du, but we'd capsize, and even if we didn't, Hunter would go crazy in this canoe all alone. He's scared to death of water."

She took her time slipping the skimpy shorts down her slim legs, balancing gracefully in the swaying conveyance. The thin gold chain and tiny gold heart were among the last things Charlie saw as she slipped into the bay.

Lou had never felt so clean in all of her life, swimming through the cool water like a convert baptized in love and forgiveness. When she swam back to shore, Charlie was there waiting, a beach towel stretched out in his hands. He wrapped her in the towel, and drew her into his warmth.

"I'll always be waiting for you," he whispered.

"Do you promise, Charlie? Do you?"

The South

Photo: Martha Dabbs Greenway

My Brother Was No Angel

Martha Dabbs Greenway

My brother was no angel, and yet angels were everywhere at his funeral.

His name was Mac. He was almost eight years older than me. I wasn't sure he even knew my name until I was a teenager and he actually expressed concern about my dating one of his friends. In the last years of his life, we enjoyed a close friendship. One of his favorite philosophies was: "You can stay home for a week and remember nothing or take a trip and gain memories for a lifetime." And, travel he did—on a motorcycle while still in high school, an F86D jet fighter plane in the Air Force, a cool looking El Camino pick-up truck to run his golf course. A man on the move, one of his last joys was a huge black Harley Davidson motorcycle. "You pay a lot of money for a sound like this," he once told me as he revved up the engine ready for another adventure on the road.

But back to the angels and his funeral …

The night before the service his family and I were doing what families do at such times—telling stories and enjoying the occasional outburst of healing laughter. When someone mentioned that Mac had given Harley jackets to his three grandsons for Christmas, they began to say with bravado, "Let's wear them to the funeral." I chimed in to say that I had a Harley jacket too, one my friend Peggy spotted at a thrift shop and bought for me. "Yeah, let's wear them!" I agreed.

The next day I stood in my conservative gray Land's End dress when the oldest grandchild sidled up to me and asked, "Aunt Mar, are you really going to wear your jacket?"

I knew it was a most important, fish-or-cut-bait, defining moment, and with only a slight hesitation, I replied, "Yes, I am because Mac would have wanted me to follow my heart."

I'm sure there were murmured comments when those three young men and their sixty-three-year-old, gray-haired great aunt entered the church, but only one person approached me following the service. "Uh, are you wearing that jacket—hmmm—because of your brother?"

I wanted to say something like, "Hell no. I wear this to all funerals," but refrained and simply said, "Yes, of course."

And, what does this have to do with angels? The Harley Davidson logo on our jackets looked like an angel's wing. Mac's middle child had ridden the Harley out and parked it beside the cemetery gate. Someone had placed a single red rose on the seat. More angel wings in the logos on the bike.

After the graveyard service, as we came out from under the funeral home tent, two people, separately, came up to me and gushed, "Did you see it? The clouds formed perfect angel wings. They came out of a clear blue sky and were visible through the entire service. Then they vanished!"

I wish I had seen those clouds but the final angel winged its way later that evening, and it seemed to be just for me.

We had opened my house for visitation and there were just two friends left chatting in the kitchen when I took a phone call and wandered into the living room while talking. What I saw there was most amazing. We had lit candles throughout the house. On the coffee table was a brass candleholder with a shield around its backside. The candle had melted in the shape of an angel's wing.

The South

The River

There is a peaceful river that flows to us from each other

We are, the two of us, united in its flow

It awakens us to our heart's desires, and liberty

As we stand here, hands held, looking deeply into each other's eyes,

We anoint each other

In this Heavenly water

We rise up from within ourselves

To fly out on to the Earth as who we really are

Spirits born anew

Free to do, and say, what is truly in our hearts

Not burdened any more with fear, doubts, shame

So many lower ego feelings

No, unchained are we in our resolve

To look no more to others for our approval

Or linger in other's disapproval of us,

Our motives and our drives

Ungainly have we become

Burdened by our heavy chains

Free now are we to soar,

To move about untethered

To glide freely to the shore of this peaceful river

That runs through us

Unites us, and most especially, sets us free

Free to do great works,

To deliver our God-given gifts

To share and care in new ways

Unencumbered by old ideas of what we couldn't be

So follow me to the shoreline

Jump in, let life flow anew in to you

Nothing will ever be the same,

And that will make all the difference.

— *Kathie Corley/Cerantha*

The South

In my South, the most treasured things

passed down from generation to

generation are the family recipes.

—Robert St. John, chef

Southern Cooking

A Drunken Chicken.

Ms. Thelma's Special Recipes

Remembered by Hugh China, Recorded by Kathy China

My husband's mother, Ms. Thelma, worked magic in the kitchen. Her fans extended well beyond her family and included attendees at the church.

"Thelma, what are you taking to church today," her husband inquired one Sunday.

"Well, Robert Lee, I made chicken and the pastor wanted chocolate cake. So I made Better Than Sex cake."

"Now, Thelma, you can't call the cake that in church."

Of course, the AME pastor raved about Ms. Thelma's special chicken and cake. "Now what do you call that chicken?" he asked.

"Well... that is my Drunken Chicken."

Robert Lee's eyes focused on his wife's.

Eyebrows raised on the pastor's face. "Why is it called that?"

Recognizing her husband's discomfort, Ms. Thelma realized she couldn't admit that the chicken was made with bourbon.

"It just has a special marinade."

"And that cake. What is the name of that cake?," the pastor asked.

Robert Lee shook his head subtly as he held Ms. Thelma's gaze.

Southern Cooking

Drunken Chicken

Ms. Thelma

1 whole frying chicken, cut into pieces
1 cup all-purpose flour (or enough to coat chicken)
2-3 cups cooking oil
About ½ cup of bourbon or rum
Seasoning of your choice

1. Wash and dry chicken.

2. Season chicken with select seasoning. Set aside and marinate for minimum of 30 minutes.

3. Place oil in a frying pan or cast iron skillet. Heat oil on medium until hot. Place flour and chicken pieces in plastic bag and shake lightly to coat chicken.

4. Cook chicken until golden brown.

5. Line sheet pan with foil. Remove chicken from oil and place in pan. Sprinkle with rum or bourbon. Wrap tight in foil and let the chicken rest. Best served warm.

Better Than Sex Cake

Ms. Thelma

Your favorite yellow cake or pound cake recipe

or 1 Duncan Hines cake mix

2 16-oz. cans crushed pineapple

2 5.1-oz. boxes vanilla pudding

whipped cream or 1 tub of Cool Whip

1 tbsp. butter

1. Bake cake in 9x13 glass pan until done.

2. While cake is baking, mix pudding according to directions and set aside.

3. About ten minutes before cake finishes, place pineapple in sauce pan with butter, heat through.

4. Remove cake from oven and spoon pineapple mixture over cake while hot. Allow the mixture to soak into cake. Then cool for at least 30 minutes.

5. Spread pudding over pineapple evenly. Cool completely.

6. Top cake with whipped cream.

Note: Cake may be pre-cut with a very sharp knife before applying whipped cream.

Southern Cooking

These recipes are from the 1950 edition of Charleston Receipts. *Charlotte Russe was a dessert that my grandmother, who was raised on Bugby Plantation, Wadmalaw Island, South Carolina, would serve at holiday dinners as a special treat! Wine jelly was always served at Sunday family dinners throughout the year.*

Charlotte Russe
Cindy Seabrook

1 pint of whipping cream
1 tsp of vanilla
5 egg whites
sherry to taste
¼ cup of cold whole milk
¼ cup warm whole milk
1/2 cup sugar
½ tbsp gelatin
Lady fingers, split

Whip cream until stiff.

Add vanilla and sugar plus sherry to taste.

Soften gelatin in cold milk then add to warm milk.

When milk mixture is cool, add to the above mixture, beating the cream all the time.

Add beaten egg whites.

Pour in a glass bowl completely lined with the split Lady Fingers.

Cover and refrigerate for at least 8 hours prior to serving.

Serves 6

Wine Jelly

Cindy Seabrook

2 envelopes gelatin
1/2 cup cold water
1 cup boiling water
2 cups sweet sherry wine
pinch of salt
1/4 cup lemon juice, strained
1/4 cup orange juice, strained
2/3 cup sugar

Soak gelatin in cold water about 10 minutes. Add boiling water; stir well; cool partially. Then add sugar, salt, lemon and orange juices and sherry wine.

My grandmother would pour mixture into individual small glass bowls. She would immediately add half of a peach to each bowl. When cool and congealed, she would top with homemade whipped cream.

It was a delicious dessert!

Five Spice Cake

Karen Chandler

1 tsp each of the following spice extracts: coconut, rum, butter, lemon, vanilla, almond (glaze, only)

2 sticks of margarine, melted

1/2 cup oil

3 cups sugar

5 eggs

3 cups all-purpose flour (sifted)

1/2 tsp baking powder (sifted)

1 cup milk

Cake

Cream the butter, oil, and sugar until fluffy.

Beat the eggs with a mixer in a bowl until yellow.

Add eggs to the butter mixture.

Combine the sifted flour and baking powder in a separate bowl.

Add the flour mix to the egg mixture alternating with milk.

Stir in the spices (except the almond).

Pour mixture into a buttered and floured bundt pan..

Bake at 325 degrees for 1-1/2 hours.

Glaze

1 cup sugar

1/2 cup of water

1 tsp each of all of the spice extracts used in the cake including the almond

Put the spices, sugar and water in a pan and boil for 2 minutes.

When the cake comes out of the oven, let it sit for 5 minutes in the pan.

Pour 1/2 of the glaze on the cake while it is in the pan and let it sit for 15 minutes.

Turn cake onto a plate and pour the remainder of the glaze over the cake.

Let it sit for 15 minutes, slice and enjoy!

Pure Sin
A Chocolate Concoction to Die For

Martha Dabbs Greenway

Southerners love desserts that are gooey, decadent, and easy to prepare. Pure Sin reminds me of the dessert my mama used to make with chocolate wafers, whipped cream and pecans. Every Thanksgiving, when the descendants of my grandfather gather at The Crossroads, Mayesville, South Carolina, I bring Pure Sin.

Ingredients
Chocolate Brownie Mix, 18 oz.
Chocolate Instant Pudding Mix, 3.9 oz.
Cool Whip, 8 oz.

Instructions
Prepare the brownies according to the instructions on the package. Crumble when cool and put half in a large Pyrex casserole dish.

Prepare the chocolate pudding according to the instructions on the package. Smooth on a layer of chocolate pudding.

Top with a layer of Cool Whip.

Repeat.

Tastes better if made the day before and refrigerated!

Southern Cooking

Company Casserole

Gloria Burg

This is my mother's recipe. Everyone loves it—especially her grandchildren!

1 pound ground beef

2-8 oz. cans of tomto sauce

1 tsp salt

8 oz. medium noodles

1 cup cottage cheese

8 oz. cream cheese

1/4 cup sour cream

1/3 cup chopped onion

1 tbsp diced green bellpepper

Brown beef in skillet. Drain off liquid.

Stir in tomato sauce and salt.

Remove from heat.

Cook noodles in boiling salted water for ten minutes. Drain.

Combine cheeses, sour cream, onions and peppers.

In a buttered casserole dish, spread half the noodles.

Cover with cheese mixture, then cover with remaining noodles.

Top with beef mixture. Bake 30- 40 mnutes at 350 degress.

Serves 6.

No Cook Refrigerator Pickles

Mary Edna Fraser

4 1/2 cups sliced pickling cucumbers
1/2 cup sliced onions
1/2 cup vinegar
1 tsp salt
1/2 cup sugar to 3/4 cups if you like sweet
1 cup water
3 cloves garlic
1 red hot pepper minced

Bring vinegar, salt, sugar, water, garlic and pepper to boil.
Add cucumbers and onions.
Pour into jars and refrigerate.
Add fresh dill to garnish.

*I start making these pickles when the first cucumbers are ripe and keep them in my
refrigerator all summer.*

Southern Cooking

Chicken Mafe

Pascale Ferraro

Originally from Senegal, but widely spread throughout West Africa, Chicken Mafe (or Chicken with Peanut Sauce) is a hearty, tasty and rich meal for the body and the soul. Although a traditional African dish, it was not brought to America through slavery, as slaves were not given access to "noble" pieces of meat, chicken or fish. Nonetheless, all the ingredients (peanuts, yams and rice) used to make this dish are a perfect fit for Lowcountry cooking.

Ingredients
2 whole chickens

1 cup crushed peanut paste (*do not use peanut butter that is too sweet, instead use crushed peanuts without any additional ingredient…available at Whole Foods Market in bulk*).

4 fresh tomatoes

2 onions, 1 clove of garlic

2 chicken bouillon cubes

salt, pepper

1 can of tomato paste

carrots and yams

2 cups of white rice

¼ cup peanut oil

Instructions

Cut the chickens in large pieces and brown them in peanut oil.

Cut the onions, the garlic and tomatoes in small pieces.

Mix the peanut paste with a little bit of water before adding it to the pan.

Bring to a broil, add salt & pepper and add the chicken bouillon cubes.

Let simmer for about 40 minutes until the sauce thickens.

Add the chicken and the vegetables.

Let simmer until the chicken and vegetables are fully cooked.

Serve with white rice.

You can add chili pepper while cooking if you like this dish a little spicy.

Southern Cooking

Shrimp in a Pumpkin (Camarão na Moranga)

Pascale Ferraro

This dish is obviously designed for a specific festive time of the year, using large bright orange pumpkins, making it a very appealing table centerpiece while serving. Small mini pumpkins can also be used for individual servings, requiring a little more work to prepare. This native Brazilian dish would be a wonderful addition to Lowcountry Cuisine as it can be prepared with the amazing shrimp that Charleston has to offer and the traditional pumpkins in the fall.

Ingredients   (serve 6)

A 6 lb pumpkin or other squash

2 lbs medium shrimp, cleaned, peeled and deveined

2 limes

2 tsp salt

1 small serrano or jalapeno chili (optional), halved and seeded

3 bay leaves

2 cups shrimp stock

2 medium onions, chopped

2 tbsp butter

2 tbsp extra-virgin olive oil

5 medium tomatoes, peeled, seeded and chopped

3 cups cream cheese

2 tbsp all-purpose flour

2 tbsp good-quality curry powder

2 tsp Tabasco sauce (optional)

3 tbsp extra-virgin olive oil

3 tbsp neutral vegetable oil

4 tbsp finely-chopped Italian parsley

Instructions

Cut a circular opening in the top of the pumpkin (as you would for a jack-o-lantern).

Using a spoon and your hands, remove all the seeds and strings from inside the pumpkin. Wash the pumpkin thoroughly inside and out, then dry the inside with paper towel.

Preheat the oven to 400 degrees.

Put the shrimp in a large mixing bowl, then add the fresh-squeezed juice of two limes, the salt, the halved chili and the bay leaves. Mix thoroughly and refrigerate for about one hour (while the pumpkin roasts).

Wrap the pumpkin in aluminum foil, place in a large baking pan, and roast in the oven for about 50 minutes. Remove from the oven and keep warm. Keep the oven on.

In a large saucepan, heat 3 tbsp each of butter and olive oil, then saute the chopped onions for a few minutes, or until the onions are transparent but not browned. Add the tomatoes and cook, stirring frequently, for a few minutes, or until the tomato begins to break down. Add the cream cheese, and combine thoroughly, making sure that the cheese has melted and combined with the other ingredients. Reserve, keeping warm.

In a mixing bowl containing the shrimp stock, whisk in the flour and continue to whisk until there are no lumps. Mix in the curry powder and optional Tabasco sauce. Stir this mixture into the cream cheese/tomato sauce, and reserve, keeping warm.

In a large frying pan, heat 3 tbsp each of olive oil and neutral vegetable oil. Remove the shrimp from the refrigerator and saute (in two batches if necessary to avoid overcrowding). Cook for a few minutes only, stirring constantly but gently, until all the shrimp have become opaque and turned pink. Do not overcook. Stir the shrimp gently in the sauce mixture.

Open the top of the pumpkin (leaving the rest of it still covered with aluminum foil). Pour the shrimp mixture into the pumpkin, filling it completely if possible. Return the filled pumpkin to the hot oven and cook for 10 minutes. Remove from the oven, remove the aluminum foil, then place the pumpkin on a large serving platter. Sprinkle the surface of the shrimp mixture with chopped parsley. Serve on a buffet table or at the center of a dining table, with a large ladle for serving the shrimp from inside the pumpkin, along with a bit of the cooked pumpkin.

Southern Cooking

Redemptive Chili

(Kine and swine rejoice! Your arteries too.)

Paul Schwarz

I concocted this vegan chili recipe for a church dinner club oyster roast. I didn't measure anything, just kept adding, but it was a hit at the party, and I must say, delicious. This recipe evolved, and allows for creative additions and subtractions at the whim of the cook. This is not rocket science, folks.

Saute the following in olive oil and cook until tender,
(*preferably in a large cast iron or an enameled pot*)

large onion chopped

green bell pepper—one large or two small —cored and chopped

garlic — several cloves - minced

mushrooms (your choice) —10 oz. or so— sliced

carrots— 6 to 8 depending on size—diced

Add 1/2 to 2/3 small can tomato paste when vegetables are soft

Mix well before adding 1 or 2 cups vegetable broth.

Add in no particular order:

chipotle chili plus adobo or chipotle powder, or neither

smoked paprika—2 tsp.

oregano—2 tsp.

chili powder—2+ tbsp

cumin—2 tsp

celery salt—2 tsp.

soy sauce or liquid aminos—1 or 2 tbsp

worchestershire, vegan— 1 or 2 tbsp

agave syrup or other sweetener —1 tbsp

balsamic vinegar —1+ tbsp

Sriracha or other hot sauce - to taste

salt

Mix well on medium heat, then add 2 cans of beans (your choice) —pinto, black, red, or any combination

Add one can diced tomatoes with juices.

The next step can be eliminated, but adds additional plant protein and meatiness: (If you prefer, add another can of beans instead)

Tempeh or 2 packages seitan sausage, etc. *(Don't be afraid of this stuff, like I used to be. It adds substance and flavor, and won't make you a sissy).* If using tempeh, they say it's best to steam in water or broth for 10 minutes, but this may be unnecessary since it's already cooked. Then crumble into a wok or skillet, and saute in a small amount of oil with chili powder. It will look like a bunch of beans. When heated and combined, add this to the pot and mix.

You could add some chopped cilantro at this point. Then bring to a slow boil. To avoid scorching, place the pot, covered, in a 350 oven for about an hour. This will allow the ingredients and flavors to combine. If you want it more liquid, add vegetable broth at this time.

Serve with condiments of your choice: avocado, salsa, cilantro, corn chips, etc.

Southern Cooking

The Music Café

Music is a moral law. It gives soul to the universe, wings to the mind, flight to the imagination, and charm and gaiety to life and to everything.
—Plato

The Music Café is a monthly gathering of Charleston musicians and friends hosted at members' homes. Everyone brings either music or a nibble to share—and sometimes both!

Susan McAdoo, performer, teacher, and pianist for the Charleston Symphony, founded Music Cafe in 2004. In Susan's own words, here is a description of her role at Café and the monthly programs:

"My role at Café is organizer, teacher, cheerleader, performer. I send out an invitation about a week ahead of time to my steadily growing list of Café friends - many of whom are just listeners and supporters. My students play at Café, so during the weeks prior we prepare for the casual performance in our lessons. During Café, after one of the adults has played, I'm thrilled to celebrate their success and cheer on their continued efforts. I'm so impressed with their bravery and willingness to share—they are such amazing people! Finally, I too perform at Café. It's important for me to be a role model for my students - just as many of my great performer-teachers were for me."

Gayle Newcomb, a pianist and long-standing Café friend, traditionally brings her festive cranberry bread to the November and December meetings.

Gayle's Cranberry Bread
Gayle Newcomb

2 cups all-purpose flour
1 cup sugar
1 & ½ tsp. baking powder
½ tsp. baking soda
½ tsp. salt
¼ cup butter
1 egg
1 tablespoon grated orange peel
¾ cup orange juice
1 & ½ cups chopped cranberries
1 & ½ cups golden raisins
1 cup chopped walnuts

In a large bowl mix together the dry ingredients. Cut in the butter till mixture is crumbly. In another bowl, stir together the egg, orange peel and orange juice. Blend the liquid mixture with the flour mixture until the flour mixture is just moistened. Fold in the fruit and nuts (separately). Spoon into a greased 9 & ½ by 5 & ¼ loaf pan with parchment paper on the bottom. Bake @ 350 degrees F oven for 60-75 minutes(or till tester comes out clean). Cool in pan for 5 minutes. Invert onto rack turning right side up.

Optional Glaze: Stir ½ tablespoon orange juice into 1 cup powdered sugar (makes enough for 2 loaves). Drizzle over the partially cooled bread. When completely cooled, store, well-wrapped for 24 hours before serving.

The recipe also makes 3 mini-loaves. Bake for 45 minutes at 350 degrees F.

Enjoy!

Southern Cooking

When McIver Watson hosts Music Café, in addition to having a case (or two!)
of wine and a Rachmaninoff Prelude on hand, he'll prepare this addictive snack.
It's a Southern treat, much like McIver himself.

Toasted Butter Pecans

McIver Watson

4 cups pecan halves
1 tbsp salt
1/4 cup butter

Melt the butter in the microwave.
Add salt and toss with the pecans.
Place on a cookie sheet and bake at 300° F for 15-20 minutes.

You probably won't have any leftovers, but if you do, put them in an airtight container for later.

Walnuts

Philosophers have said that we love music
because it resembles the sphere-sounds of union.

We have been part of a harmony before,
so these moments of treble and bass
keep our remembering fresh.

Hearing the sound, we gather strength.
Love kindles with melody, Music feeds a lover
composure, and provides form for the imagination.
Music breathes on personal fire and makes it keener.

The waterhole is deep. A thirsty man climbs
a walnut tree growing next to the pool
and drops walnuts in one by one.

He listens carefully to the sound
as they hit and watches the bubbles.

A more rational man gives advice, You will regret
doing this. You are so far from the water
that by the time you get down to gather walnuts,
the water will have carried them away.

He replies, I am not here for walnuts.
I want the music they make when they hit.

I am so small I can barely be seen.
How can this great love be inside me?

Look at your eyes. They are so small,
but they see enormous things.

A poem by Rumi read at one of the Music Cafés.

Southern Cooking

Artists Dinner
in Chef David Vagasky's Greenhouse

Sunday, April 23, 2015

Event Time 5:00 PM

Hors D'oeuvres under the pecan tree

Arrival smoothie

New potatoes stuffed salmon cream cheese

Marinated asparagus wrapped in prosciutto

Deep fried oysters

Dinner in the Greenhouse

Salad

Compostinmyshoe lettuce with roasted tomatoes, feta cheese

and white balsamic dressing

Dinner

Mixed grill (Grilled Scallop, Beef tenderloin)

Tri-colored quinoa

Garden picked vegetables

Dessert

Chocolate tart

(With the back drop of 40 knot winds and buckets of rain, much wine and food was consumed)

Key Lime Pie

Chef David Vagasky

KEY LIME FILLING
(Yields 2 – 9 inch pies)

Ingredients
egg yolks—10 each
key lime juice—10 oz
sweet condensed milk 4—14 oz can

Directions
Blend together the ingredients listed.
Pour into your prepared graham cracker crust.
Bake at 350°F for 15-20 minutes.
Chill and serve.

BASIC CRUMB CRUST
(Yields: 14 oz, two deep dish 9" shells)

graham cracker crumbs 8 oz
granulated sugar 4 oz
butter, melted 2 oz

Method of Production:
1. Combine the graham cracker crumbs and sugar in a mixing bowl.
2. Add the melted butter and combine until evenly mixed.
3. Press the mixture into the bottoms of the pie pans.
4. Bake the shells at 350°F until the crumbs have toasted slightly and the crust has firmed.
5. Cool the shells to room temperature.
6. Fill the parbaked shells as desired.

Southern Cooking

Christmas Eggnog
Nancy J. Padgett

These eggnog recipes were passed down from my grandparents, Cyril and Frieda Mae Rutland Jones, who lived in Batesburg, just west of Columbia, South Carolina. They were famous for their Christmas-time eggnog parties.

Grandfather Jones' version for the back-room (men only).
Per 6 oz cup, or punch cup size

1 egg
1 tbsp or more powdered sugar
2 tbsp rum or more
1 tbsp Brandy, or more. Important to use good brandy.
4 oz heavy cream
Separate egg. Mix it in with other ingredients. Whip egg white and fold in, saving a dollop for the top to produce the requisite "white mustache." Grandfather Jones was reputed to have made the initial cup or so very strong, and then cut back on the liquor after the men had gotten pretty drunk.

Grandmother Jones' recipe for the Baptist Church Ladies:
Per 6 oz cup

1 egg
1 tbsp or more powdered sugar
1/2 tsp vanilla
4 oz heavy cream
Separate egg. Mix it in with other ingredients. Whip egg white and fold in. Ladies didn't get the dollop on top as the white mustache would ruin one's make-up. Grandmother Jones was known to have added 1 tsp of brandy if the preacher was not going to be present. One time the preacher discovered Grandfather Jones' "back room" but family folk lore is mum on whether he joined in or ran the sinners out of the room.

My heart-healthy recipe

per two cups—6 oz each

1 egg per two cups
2 tbsp powdered sugar or to taste
1 tsp vanilla
4 oz of half and half and 8 oz 2% milk. Total 12 oz.
Rum and brandy to taste.
Important to use good brandy as cheap brandy will taste terrible in this concoction.
I don't know if the quality of the rum matters or not. These days folks like cock-
tails and hard liquor a lot, so I use the same proportions as Grandfather Jones. For
children and others who don't drink hard liquor, I make a separate batch without the
liquor.

How much to fix:

You might think people will want only one 6 oz cup, maybe two, but we have found
most people want 3-4 cups, especially if you have a yummy salty appetizer to eat with
it. The hardest part is getting someone to separate all those eggs. My husband is an
unsung hero here. I have not tried those ready-made egg whites from the grocery
store.

Variations: I have not used whiskey instead of rum, but I did substitute the liqueur
Tuaca, which has a light vanilla flavor, for brandy when I once ran out of brandy.
Don't use the ready-made Eggnog from the grocery store and try to doctor that up.
That result just gives Southern eggnog a bad reputation.

Southern Cooking

Pita Crisps

Louise Dabbs Bevan

3 tbsp olive oil

¾ tsp cumin

¼ tsp red pepper

5 (5-6") wheat or white pitas

1/4 cup coarsely grated Parmesan cheese.

Heat oven to 350 degrees. Mix with fork olive oil, cumin, pepper. Split pitas in half, brush with mixture. Sprinkle with cheese (and salt if you'd like) and bake 12-14 minutes or until golden. Can be stored in plastic bag for a week.

Cranberry Chutney

Louise Dabbs Bevan

3 small oranges

4 cups cranberries

2 cups sugar

1 cup chopped unpeeled apple

¼ cup seedless raisins

¼ cup chopped walnuts

½ cup orange juice or water

1 tbsp. vinegar

½ tsp ginger

½ tsp cinnamon

Cut oranges in halves, scoop out 1 cup segments. In 2-quart saucepan combine all ingredients, bring to boil and then simmer, stirring frequently until cranberries have popped and mixture reaches desired thickness.

Southern Cooking

Hoppin' John

A Lowcountry New Year's Day Tradition

Myra Yeatts

This black-eyed peas and rice dish originated in the South Carolina Lowcountry. African-Americans who worked on the rice plantations in the 1800s are given credit for this tasty concoction.

The peas represent peace and the rice promises riches. The story is that a street vendor, a crippled Black man named Hoppin' John, first sold this dish in Charleston in the mid-1800s. Since then, it has taken on the significance of a good luck charm for the New Year.

An additional touch is to bury a shiny new dime in the dish of peas and rice. The lucky diner who finds the dime in his/her serving of Hoppin' John can be assured prosperity in the coming year.

Ingredients:

2 cups dried black-eyed peas
1 lb of ham hocks
1 tbsp. of bacon grease
1 chopped onion
3 cloves of minced garlic
1 tsp. of salt
4 cups of chicken stock
2 cups of uncooked rice

Rinse and drain black-eyed peas. Cover with water in a large pot. Bring to a boil, remove from heat, cover and let them stand for a couple of hours. Drain and rinse once more.

Use bacon grease to sauté onions and garlic. Add to drained peas. Add chicken stock, ham hocks and salt. Cook over medium heat for two hours.

Stir in rice, cover and cook for 20 minutes.

The final dish will be tender and powerful for the future of six to eight people.

Best served with collard greens and corn bread.

Happy New Year!

Southern Cooking

Creativity is always a leap of faith.

You're faced with a blank page,

blank easel, or an empty stage.

—Julia Cameron

Writers
Artists
Chefs

NANCY ALPERT grew up in the libraries and department stores of Southern California. She emigrated to the Bay Area, graduated from Stanford then Berkeley, and spent twenty years in geriatric social work. Since the age of twelve, Nancy's filled her journals with pure poetry—as well as some poems. Her travel essays appear in the anthologies *Venturing in Italy: Travels in Puglia, Land between Two Seas* (Traveler's Tales), *Wandering in Costa Rica — Landscapes Lost and Found*, and *Wandering in Bali — A Tropical Paradise Discovered* (Wanderland Writers). On Thanksgiving 2013, the *Baltimore Sun* printed her humorous Op-Ed, "The Four Questions of Thanksgivikkuh" (and Nancy's essay, "Spending the High Holidays in Bali" can be found at ReformJudaism.org.) Nancy shares her home with her fourteen-year-old daughter/editor; cats and dog—Donut, Cupcake and Latke—and an undomesticated Muse.

CHERYL ARMSTRONG is a San Francisco Bay Area writer, photographer, certified yoga instructor, and world traveler who writes novels, stories and essays. Her career was spent as an automation librarian in academic, public and special libraries. She was a Peace Corps volunteer in Ethiopia and Eritrea, and a librarian in Istanbul, Turkey. Cheryl writes about outsiders and what they teach us about ourselves.

UNITY BARRY graduated from the San Francisco Art Institute, but after she worked her way too long in the corporate world, she retired to write about her favorite subjects—artists and Paris during the Gilded Age. She recently finished her first historical novel, *Luminous—Berthe Marisot and the Birth of Impressionism* and is starting her next about Rosa Bonheur. She was a short-listed finalist in the 2011 William Faulkner-William Wisdom Writing Competition and has two short pieces in the anthologies, *Wandering in Paris, Luminaries* and *Love in the City of Light* and *Wandering in Cornwall: Mystery, Mirth and Transformation in the Land of the Ancient Celts*.

LOUISE DABBS BEVAN, beloved Mayor of Dabbs Crossroads and a strong advocate of highways devoid of litter and excess signage, received early assertiveness training by standing her ground with five brothers--three older and two younger. Her interests include restoration of historical sites, musical performances and lively conversations. She has a degree in music from Duke University with further training at Julliard School, and serves as a substitute organist at Salem Black River Presbyterian Church, Mayesville, South Carolina.

CAROLYN BISHOP-McLEOD, born in Charleston, South Carolina, developed her appreciation for diversity and adventure growing up in New Jersey, Idaho, and Hawaii. A social worker for over thirty years, she was an advocate for victims of oppression, racism, domestic violence and child sexual abuse. Now she nurtures her feline "children." Always grateful for her deep southern roots, she cheers for the Clemson Tigers and feels at home in the Lowcountry.

ALPHONSO BROWN, born and reared in Rantowles, South Carolina, a rural area outside of Charleston, South Carolina, has received numerous degrees, but is perhaps best known as the director of five choirs and the band at Mount Zion AME Church, and his Gullah Tours of Charleston. The author of *A Gullah Guide to Charleston*, Alphonso charms natives and visitors who want to discover the "real" Charleston.

GLORIA BURG, an interior designer born and raised in Columbia, South Carolina, began her love and fascination with cooking in the late 60's. Coming from a family of good cooks with Lebanese and Greek heritage, it was natural to branch out into other cuisines—French and Italian from a life of travel and Southern from her roots. Gloria has taken cooking classes with Jacques Pepin, Marion Sullivan and Nathalie Dupree.

MARY BRENT CANTARUTTI, born, bred and reared to be a fan-carrying lady, headed west in pursuit of romance and adventure. She never lost her drawl. Co-founder of the Southern Sampler Artists Colony and writer of Southern Women's Fiction, her inner compass points toward cooling Atlantic breezes. Her first novel, *The Bottle Tree*, was a short-listed finalist in the Novel-in-Progress category of the 2010 William Faulkner-William Wisdom Creative Writing Competition, as well as a finalist in the Novel category in 2011.

TONI CARREIRO, formerly a product manager for Levi Strauss & Co., San Francisco, went on to become a website designer, but she never lost her passion for fiber art. An avid knitter and seamstress, she just bought her dream sewing machine, a Bernina. Always eager for a challenge, she enjoys sharing her fiber art discoveries at tonicarrdesigns.com. Toni lives in San Rafael, California, with her husband, grown son, and the love of her life, "Ollie," a sassy poodle.

KAREN CHANDLER, Associate Professor in Arts Management at the College of Charleston, received her Ph.D. in Studies in Arts and Humanities from New York University, M.A. in music education from Columbia University-Teachers College in New York, and B.S. in music education from Hampton University. From 2001-2004, she served as director of the College of Charleston's Avery Research Center for African American History and Culture. Co-founder of the Charleston Jazz Initiative, a multi-year study of the jazz tradition in Charleston and South Carolina, Karen has been widely recognized for her passion and dedication to the arts, including being presented the 2010 Preserving Our Places in History Individual Award by the South Carolina African American Heritage Commission.

KATHY CHINA lives in Sumter, South Carolina with her chef husband, a Siamese cat, and two horses. Born and raised in North Dakota, she moved to Sumter after college to pursue a career in law enforcement, primarily serving in the Mounted Patrol Division. For the past fifteen years she has been self-employed as a massage therapist, fitness trainer, and yoga instructor (now registered at 500-hour level). Writing is a passion she pursues in her spare time.

TY COLLINS, a retired professor of English and Theatre, studied drama with Lee Strasberg (NYC), and also took master classes taught by Elia Kazan and Sidney Kingsley (Actors Studio). He is a former theatre manager for the Negro Ensemble Company (NYC), Joe Papp's Public Theatre, The New York Shakespeare Festival, and The Big Apple Circus at Lincoln Center. As a visual artist, his studio training includes The Barnes Foundation in Merion, Pennsylvania, and the Art Students' League in NYC. As an independent producer/director, he is a writer/collaborator of new plays for the theatre. Currently, Ty does reenactments at Middleton Place Historic Site in Charleston, South Carolina.

JOANNA CROWELL is the founder of Ascension Theatre and the Women Writing from Experience workshop series in Charleston, South Carolina. A professional actress for over twenty years, she has performed her own poetry across Canada and the United States. A strong advocate for women, social justice, and peace, she is the author of the choreopoem *Double Dutch: What are you so afraid of? Jump in!* and the play *AWOL: A Soldier's Journey*. Her first collection of poems, *I Ate a Rainbow for Breakfast*, was published in 2012. She currently resides on Johns Island, South Carolina.

SHARON COOPER-MURRAY (The Gullah Lady), born and raised in rural Lake City, South Carolina, learned to quilt at a young age and be wary of "haints" and "hags." Sharon's introduction to the Gullah people, language and culture happened on vacation in 1978. It was on a sea island named Wadmalaw, a world apart, located just southwest of Charleston, South Carolina—and inhabited by Gullah people, descendants of West Africans imported as slave labor for Lowcountry rice and indigo plantations. Captivated by the setting and close-knit community, Sharon learned the Creole Gullah language, the waning art of rag quilting, and fueled her passion for traditional Gullah music and food customs. Sharon's proven commitment to the preservation and increased awareness of all things Gullah inspired the creation of *De Gullah Enna Pry* in 1997 and The Community Rag Quilting Preservation Initiative in 2011. A Speech and Drama graduate of Knoxville College, Knoxville, Tennessee, she is a widely acclaimed storyteller and textile artist. Sharon lives in Charleston, South Carolina, where she presents the Gullah culture—stories, songs, legends and crafts—to an ever-expanding audience at home . . . and beyond.

KATHIE CORLEY/CERANTHA, a passionate Native American style flute player and instructor, is a gifted Shaman, Reiki Master, writer, and painter. She expresses her varied spiritually endowed interests in her writings, music, workshops, and sound energy work.

WILLIAM ALEXANDER (BILLY) DABBS (1923-2013) grew up in the Salem Black River community near Mayesville, South Carolina. A Navy pilot in World War II, in 1943 he married his childhood sweetheart, Lynda Louise Corbett of Mayesville. Together they raised four children. A constant reader with a keen curiosity about every facet of life, he was a consummate storyteller, quick to entertain others with his humorous recollections.

MAUREEN DIXON was born in the suburbs of Los Angeles and hopscotched her way up the California coast until she settled in the San Francisco Bay Area. A writer by avocation, she entered the field penning journals, short stories and poems. She is the author of *Conversations With Dad*, based on her father's stories of his life in the 1930s, '40s and '50s, and is currently co-authoring the memoir of a young Afghan boy whose hero's journey leads him through challenges in American foster care. Maureen is board chair of WriterCoach Connection, a nonprofit whose mission is to help close the achievement gap for middle and high school students in the areas of critical thinking and clear writing.

ANTON DUMARS, a thirty-five year resident of Folly Beach and a US Navy submarine veteran, serves as a geology adjunct professor at the College of Charleston and a Coastal Scientist for Tideline Consulting, LLC. Mostly he likes showing off the South Carolina salt marsh to guests aboard his tour boat, "Tideline".

Artists Writers Chefs

PASCALE FERRARO is a French girl who grew up and worked in tourism in West Africa and Indian Ocean, as well as Brazil, before following the love of her life to the United States. A nomad, a citizen of the world with a true passion for travel and meeting people, she recently settled in the vineyards of Burgundy, France but that was not enough. On the road again, in search of another anchor point, she fell in love with Charleston and its wonders—the seaside, the sun, the festivals and the people. There is no place like Home!

MARY EDNA FRASER is a South Carolina artist whose pioneering work has been collected and exhibited worldwide in more than one hundred solo exhibitions. Her large-scale silk batiks (an ancient resist process using wax and dye on cloth) feature aerial landscapes, deep ocean waterscapes, and outer space imagery. Environmental awareness is the common thread in her career of four decades NASA recognized Mary Edna as their Artist of the Year in 1995, and she was featured demonstrating batik at the Smithsonian Folklife Festival, District of Columbia. National Geographic and Turner Broadcasting have broadcast her endeavors. Beginning with the bird's eye view of her grandfather's vintage 1946 Ercoupe plane, she has photographed and always seen the bigger picture. Science has become more beautiful and accessible through the lens of Mary Edna Fraser's art. She welcomes visitors to her James Island Creek studio. www.maryedna.com.

HARLAN GREENE, Charleston history editor and the head of Special Collections of the College of Charleston's Addlestone Library, is quick to proclaim his "unabashed love for his native city." He has published three novels and several nonfiction books about Charleston and Lowcountry history.

MARTHA DABBS GREENWAY is a seventh generation South Carolinian and resides at Dabbs Cross-roads in a rambling country farm house built by her granddaddy. Co-founder of Southern Sampler Artists Colony and retired Director of the Sumter County Cultural Commission, Martha lives contently with her two cats, Sonoma, rescued on the Northern California coast and Salem, an orange tabby, who showed up on her porch, while she was reading about an orange cat dropped off at a library in Iowa.

ANN LANGSTON, a San Francisco Bay Area artist whose work is inspired by travel and immersion in foreign cultures, feels a deep connection to Pawleys Island, South Carolina. Her April refuge for more than forty years, she loves to paint the old cottages on the island, each holding treasured stories of families, who for generations, have gathered there by the sea.

SUSAN McADOO, pianist for the Charleston Symphony Orchestra Chorus, holds performance degrees from Westminster Choir College, Princeton, New Jersey (Master of Music) and University of North Carolina, Chapel Hill (Bachelor of Arts). A solo and collaborative pianist, teacher, vocal coach and choir director, she has performed at Spoleto Festival, USA, as well as numerous concerts throughout the East Coast and in Europe, South Korea and China. In 2004 she founded, and has since been the director of, Music Café, a monthly Charleston soirée for adult amateur musicians.

LINDA WATANABE McFERRIN is an award-winning poet, travel writer, and novelist. Her latest novel, *Dead Love*, was a Bram Stoker Award Finalist. Linda has judged the San Francisco Literary Awards, the Josephine Miles Award for Literary Excellence and the Kiriyama Prize, served as a visiting mentor for the Loft Mentor Series and been guest faculty at the Oklahoma Arts Institute. A past NEA Panelist and juror for the Marin Literary Arts Council and the founder of Left Coast Writers®, she has led workshops in the United States, Greece, France, Italy, Ireland, Central America, and Indonesia.

BENTE MIROW grew up in Denmark and has worked as a freelance writer for twenty-five years. Before settling in California, she spent fifteen years traveling the world while pursuing a career in the airline industry, as well as steering sailboats into the wind. Somewhere along the way she received a Master's degree in Humanities, which sparked her interest in fiction and non-fiction. The past four years, she authored elementary school curriculums for social-emotional life skills books. Visiting the real South with the SSAC writers was a mind-altering experience for this writer from the real North.

GAYLE NEWCOMB, a grateful and proud member of the Charleston Music Café, is also a James Island gardener and watercolor, collage and fiber artist.

CATHLEEN O'BRIEN is a fifth generation Californian and book designer by profession. She fell in love with the writings of the South in college when she was lucky to take a course in Southern Literature. Her newest passion is botanicals—which she captures on paper with pencil, pen and watercolors. Can there really be 50,000,000 cells in a single leaf? She received her Master Artist in Botanical Illustration Certificate in 2015 and sells and exhibits her botanicals in the San Francisco Bay Area.

NANCY J. PADGETT was born and raised in Walterboro, South Carolina., and traces her Southern lineage to the early 18th century. She graduated from Emory University, Atlanta, Georgia, and then migrated to California, where she received her Ph.D. in history from Stanford University, Menlo Park. Her study of the ancient Etruscans and Romans led to her interest in storytelling—specifically how it shapes memory and history. She returns to South Carolina often, and enjoys spinning family "tales" around the supper table.

MARY JEAN (MJ) PRAMIK moonlights as a medical writer, contributes to Travelers' Tales "Venturing in" series on the Canal du Midi, and Southern Greece and Ireland, and anthologies on Costa Rica, Bali, and Cornwall, England. She's won Solas Travel Writing awards for her travel essays, blogs about travel and science at *Field Notes: Travel in Times of Catastrophic Change* (http://www.mjpramik.com), and recently traveled to Cuba, Ohio, Japan, Peru, and Morocco.

CATHERINE PYKE finds women philanthropists colorful and compelling. Her fascination was sparked by her nearly thirty-year career as a program officer for the Hearst Foundations. The tapestry of her interests also weaves in the founders of the college and university that she loves: Scripps College and Stanford University. She is currently writing a narrative non-fiction book about the lives and legacies of Phoebe Hearst, Jane Stanford and Ellen Browning Scripps.

CINDY RASICOT is a free-lance writer, former psychotherapist, and adoptive mother living in the Bay Area. She was raised on black-eyed peas and fried chicken in Aiken, South Carolina. Although her family moved to California when she was ten, she still shares a love of all things Southern. She currently works at Community Options for Families and Youth as a Clinical Case Manager.

CINDY SEABROOK moved to Charleston when she was five years old, but her father's family landed on these shores in the early 1700's. Even though she has lived in other places, she always finds her way back to Charleston, a city she loves for its rich culture. When she isn't enjoying the art, music, drama—and food—she gardens.

Artists Writers Chefs

PAUL SCHWARZ, a native of Saint Louis, Missouri, completed his undergraduate education at Grinnell College, Grinnell, Iowa, and graduated from Washington University Medical School, Saint Louis. He served in the US Army in Vietnam and had a medical practice in Fort Smith, Arkansas for 35 years. He also attended Shelter Institute, Bath, Maine and subsequently built, by himself, an "eco compound" (two buildings) in the mountains of North West Arkansas. Retired, he moved to Charleston—"the center of the earth," according to Paul—in 2008, right after Hurricane Hugo, and happily undertook the restoration of his beloved Charleston "single house," which dates to 1890.

ANNE SIGMON is Virginia born and southern bred. She grew up loving blue crab, Virginia ham, and Georgia pecan pie. Moving west after college, she lost her drawl but gained a love of adventure travel. A stroke survivor, Anne writes about stroke and autoimmune disease (at AnneSigmon.com) as well as adventure travel for people with health concerns (at JunglePants.com). Anne's work appears regularly in magazines and travel anthologies, most recently *Wandering in Cornwall: Mystery, Mirth and Transformation in the Land of the Ancient Celts* (August 2015), and *Bradt Guide's To Oldly Go* (November 2015).

CHEF DAVID VAGASKY's passion for the culinary arts evolved from his Minnesota heritage. A 1986 graduate of the Culinary Institute of America, David was introduced to the tantalizing world of chocolate during his internship at The Greenbrier resort in White Sulphur Springs, West Virginia. In 1989 David opened St. Johns Island Café on Johns Island, South Carolina, a popular full-service café with an in-house bakery. Sixteen years later, he left the restaurant business to teach in the Pastry Department of the Culinary Institute of Charleston. An educator andchocolatier extraordinaire, David enjoys the slow paced, Lowcountry lifestyle.

WILLIAM HARRISON (BILLY) VANDIVER is a native of Charleston and a graduate of the College of Charleston, retired from a career in education at both Trident Technical College and the Medical University of South Carolina, Charleston. A tour guide by nature, he enjoys introducing visitors to Charleston's history, gardens, and architectural diversity—and always knows where to find the tastiest fried oysters in town!

McIVER WATSON is "Da laud and pro-tector at 84 Pitt Street of all chulluns and animals."

MYRA YEATTS wears her Southern culture with both pride and irreverence, a paradox that often defines her writing. For years she made favorable impressions on young men who had made bad decisions as she taught English at Wateree Correctional Institute.

Photo: Cathleen O'Brien

Previously published by SSAC Press

🌿 *"Like improvised jazz riffs, A Southern Sampler*
is a cultural arts masterpiece that resonates with
the soul of the American South."

—Karen Chandler, Professor in Arts Management,
College of Charleston, and Co-founder of the
Charleston Jazz Initiative

A Southern Sampler can be ordered on Amazon.

34534815R00087

Made in the USA
San Bernardino, CA
31 May 2016